ONE THOUSAND WORDS

**that you must know for
standardized tests,
high school,
university,
and life!**

Charles Gulotta

One Thousand Words

This is the first edition.

ISBN-13: 978-0-9653263-6-0
ISBN-10: 0-9653263-6-5

Mostly Bright Ideas
www.mostlybrightideas.com

√ **ABASE** (uh-BASE) *verb* — **to lower or reduce in rank; degrade**
    Other forms: Abased (*adj*); abasement *(noun)*
    Sentence: His criminal actions *abased* the reputation of the entire company.

√ **ABATE** (uh-BATE) *verb* — **to decrease in intensity; to lessen**
    Other forms: Abated (*adj*); abatement *noun*)
    Sentence: They waited in the shelter until the storm *abated*.

√ **ABDICATE** (AB-dih-kate) *verb* — **to relinquish or surrender; to disown**
    Other form: Abdication *(noun)*
    Sentence: The king refused to *abdicate* the throne, and had to be removed by force.

√ **ABDUCT** (ab-DUKT) *verb* — **to carry away a person by force; to kidnap**
    Other form: Abduction *(noun)*
    Sentence: Thousands of people are *abducted* every year and sold into slavery.

ABERRATION (ab-er-AY-shun) *noun* — **something outside of what is normal or expected**
    Other form: Aberrational *(adj)*
    Sentence: Her failing grade on the math test was an *aberration*; she was a top student.

✗ **ABET** (uh-BET) *verb* — **to encourage or assist**
    Other form: Abetment *(noun)*
    Sentence: Because he drove the getaway car, he was convicted of *abetting* the robbers.

✗ **ABEYANCE** (uh-BAY-ents) *noun* — **a temporary inactivity; suspension**
    Other form: Abeyant *(adj)*
    Sentence: I kept the wild dog in *abeyance* by offering it food.

√ **ABHOR** (ab-HOR) *verb* — **to hate intensely; loathe**
    Other forms: Abhorrence *(noun);* abhorrently *(adv)*
    Sentence: The brothers enjoyed wrestling, but *abhorred* real violence.

√ **ABIDE** (uh-BIDE) *verb* — **to allow or tolerate**
    Other form: Abiding *(adj)*
    Sentence: The teacher could no longer *abide* the student's rudeness.

√ **ABJECT** (AB-jekt) *adj* — **in a low or poor condition; cast down**
Other forms: Abjection (*noun*); abjectly *(adv))*
Sentence: Penniless and hungry, the woman had been reduced to *abject* suffering.

√ **ABJURE** (ab-JOOR) *verb* — **to formally renounce; to reject a position or belief**
Other form: Abjuration (*noun*)
Sentence: Once on trial, he *abjured* his gang's violent philosophy.

ABRIDGE (uh-BRIJ) *verb* — **to condense or shorten, especially a literary work**
Other form: Abridgement (*noun*)
Sentence: The *abridged* version of the novel was missing some important scenes.

√ **ABROGATE** (AB-roh-gate) *verb* — **to annul or discontinue; abolish**
Other form: Abrogation (*noun*)
Sentence: The people rejoiced when their queen *abrogated* the harsh tax.

√ **ABSCOND** (ab-SKOND) *verb* — **to depart secretly; to hide**
Other form: Abscondence (*noun*)
Sentence: Utterly humiliated, the overthrown dictator *absconded* to a remote island.

ABSOLUTION (ab-suh-LOO-shun) *noun* — **forgiveness; releasing from guilt or sin**
Other form: Absolve (*verb*)
Sentence: Guilt can cause us to seek *absolution* through good works.

ABSOLVE (ab-ZOLV) *verb* — **to free from guilt or responsibility; to acquit**
Other form: Absolution (*noun*)
Sentence: The sympathetic jury *absolved* the accused man of all responsibility.

√ **ABSTAIN** (ab-STANE) *verb* — **to refuse to participate; to refrain**
Other forms: Abstemious (*adj*); abstinence (*noun*)
Sentence: Determined to lose weight, she *abstained* from all desserts for a year..

ABUT (uh-BUT) *verb* — **to border; to have at least one point of contact**
Other forms: Abutment (*noun*); abutting (*adj*)
Sentence: Our land *abutted* the national park, so we had few neighbors.

✓ **ACCEDE** (ak-SEED) *verb* — **to express approval; to give consent**
Other form: Accession *(noun)*
Sentence: We were happy about the sale and *acceded* to all of the buyer's requests.

ACCENTUATE (ak-SEN-choo-wate) *verb* — **to highlight, accent, or stress**
Other form: Accentuation *(noun)*
Sentence: The comedian *accentuated* the punchlines with his own laughter.

✓ **ACCOST** (uh-KAWST) *verb* — **to approach aggressively and without invitation**
Other form: Accostable *(adj)*
Sentence: The movie star was afraid of being *accosted* by fans, and rarely left the house.

ACCRETION (uh-KREE-shun) *noun* — **the gathering of objects over time; collection**
Other forms: Accrete *(verb)*; accretionary *(adv)*
Sentence: Saturn's rings are an *accretion* of rocks, pebbles, and dust.

ACUMEN (ah-KYOO-men) *noun* — **sharpness of mind; shrewdness**
Other form: Acuminous *(adj)*
Sentence: The experienced chess player's *acumen* overwhelmed the novice.

ACUTE (uh-KYOOT) *adj* — **sharp; intense; urgent**
Other forms: Acuteness *(noun)*; acutely *(adv)*
Sentence: The pain in his side was *acute*, and he was rushed to surgery.

ADHERE (ad-HEER) *verb* — **to follow or agree with; stick to**
Other form: Adherence *(noun)*
Sentence: I *adhered* to the itinerary, afraid of getting lost in a strange country.

ADHERENT (ad-HEER-ent) *noun* — **a believer, follower, or advocate of a particular idea or set of ideas**
Other form: Adherently *(adv)*
Sentence: As an *adherent* of an orthodox religion, he could not eat certain foods.

ADMONISH (ad-MAHN-ish) *verb* — **to express warning or disapproval, especially for the purpose of encouragement or instruction**
Other form: Admonishment *(noun)*
Sentence: Dissatisfied with my work, the teacher admonished me in front of everyone.

5

ADORN (uh-DORN) *verb* — **to decorate**
 Other form: Adornment *(noun)*
 Sentence: The house was *adorned* with flowers for the wedding.

ADULATION (ah-JOO-lay-shun) *noun* — **enthusiastic praise; excessive devotion**
 Other form: Adulate *(verb)*
 Sentence: The opera singer was in tears as the audience showered her with *adulation*.

ADVERSE (AD-verse) *adj* — **hostile; unfavorable; opposite in position**
 Other form: Adversity *(noun)*
 Sentence: Despite the *adverse* conditions on the mountain, we reached the peak safely.

ADVERSITY (ad-VERS-ih-tee) *noun* — **a condition of suffering or bad fortune**
 Other forms: Adverse *(adj)*; adversely *(adv)*
 Sentence: Sometimes *adversity* is the best teacher.

AESTHETIC (ess-THET-ik) *adj* — **involving a sensuous appreciation of beauty**
 Other form: Aesthetically *(adv)*
 Sentence: We appreciated the play's *aesthetic* appeal, but had no idea what it was about.

AFFINITY (uh-FIN-uh-tee) *noun* — **a special attraction or relationship; kinship**
 Other form: Affinitive *(adj)*
 Sentence: My grandmother had an *affinity* for cats, and always had at least two.

AFFLUENT (AFF-loo-ent) *adj* — **having an abundance; wealthy**
 Other form: Affluence *(noun)*
 Sentence: Their big house and fancy car made us think they were *affluent*.

AFFRONT (uh-FRUNT) *noun* — **a deliberately offensive or insulting act or statement**
 Other form: Affront *(verb)*
 Sentence: Your words are an *affront* to me, and I demand an apology.

AGGRANDIZE (uh-GRAN-dyze) *verb* — **to make greater, at least in appearance; exalt**
 Other form: Aggrandizement *(noun)*
 Sentence: Never satisfied, the dictator continued to *aggrandize* his palace for many years.

AGGRAVATE (AGG-ruh-vate) *verb* — **to make worse or more severe**
  Other form: Aggravation *(noun)*
  Sentence: War often *aggravates* the difficult conditions in which people live.

AGGREGATE (AGG-ruh-git) *noun* — **cluster; collection; sum**
  Other form: Aggregation *(noun)*
  Sentence: London is an *aggregate* of individuals from all over the world.

AGILE (AH-jil) *adj* — **able to move quickly and gracefully**
  Other form: Agility *(noun)*
  Sentence: A ballet dancer must be both *agile* and strong.

ALACRITY (uh-LAK-rih-tee) *noun* — **speed; eagerness; readiness**
  Other form: Alacritous *(adj)*
  Sentence: She responded to our request with *alacrity* and the job was soon done.

ALCOVE (AL-kove) *noun* — **a small room leading to a larger one; niche**
  Sentence: Our host met us in the *alcove*, then escorted us into the banquet hall.

ALIAS (AIL-ee-us) *noun* — **an assumed name**
  Other form: Alias *(adverb)*
  Sentence: The criminal was wanted by the police under five different *aliases*.

ALLAY (uh-LAY) *verb* — **to reduce in intensity; to abate**
  Other form: Allayment *(noun)*
  Sentence: The captain's calm manner served to *allay* our fears

ALLEGE (uh-LEJ) *verb* — **to state or accuse without complete proof**
  Other form: Alleged *(adj);* allegedly *(adv)*
  Sentence: After *alleging* that the man had fired a gun, the witness changed her story.

ALLEVIATE (uh-LEE-vee-ate) *verb* — **to make easier; lighten; relieve**
  Other form: Alleviation *(noun)*
  Sentence: Winning the lottery certainly helped *alleviate* his financial troubles.

ALLOY (AL-oy) *noun* — **a mixture of two or more metals**
    Other form: Alloy *(verb)*
    Sentence: As it turned out, the cup was made of an *alloy*, and was not pure gold.

AMALGAMATE (uh-MAL-guh-mate) *verb* — **to enter into a union; to combine**
    Other form: Amalgamated *(adj)*; amalgamation *(noun)*
    Sentence: The farmers formed an *amalgamation* to help reduce operating costs.

AMBROSIAL (am-BROZH-uhl) *adj* — **pleasing to the senses; divine**
    Other form: Ambrosia *(noun)*
    Sentence: The weather during the cruise was gloriously *ambrosial*.

AMENABLE (uh-MEN-uh-bull) *adj* — **capable of submission; obedient; responsive**
    Other forms: Amenability *(noun)*; amenably *(adv)*
    Sentence: The hostage was *amenable* to anything that would help him avoid more pain.

AMENITY (uh-MEN-ih-tee) *noun* — **something that produces pleasure or convenience**
    Sentence: The hotel had all the *amenities* we wanted, including a pool and health club.

AMIABLE (AY-mee-uh-bull) *adj* — **good-natured; friendly**
    Other forms: Amiability *(noun)*; amiably *(adv)*
    Sentence: We were expecting a mean and angry person, but she was extremely *amiable*.

AMICABLE (AH-mik-uh-bull) *adj* — **displaying friendship and good will**
    Other forms: Amicability *(noun)*; amicably *(adv)*
    Sentence: The negotiations began *amicably*, but they had now turned hostile.

AMOROUS (AH-mer-uss) *adj* — **expressing or feeling love**
    Other forms: Amorousness *(noun)*; amorously *(adv)*
    Sentence: When he read her letter, it sparked *amorous* feelings in him once again.

ANACHRONISM (uh-NAK-ruh-nizm) *noun* — **something chronologically out of place**
    Other form: Anachronistic *(adj)*
    Sentence: A brontosaurus in modern-day Tokyo would be an *anachronism*.

ANALGESIC (an-ul-JEE-zik) *adj* — **removing sense of pain without loss of consciousness**
Other forms: Analgesia, analgesic *(nouns)*
Sentence: Many people claim acupuncture has effective *analgesic* qualities.

ANECDOTE (AH-nek-dote) *noun* — **an interesting or amusing incident, told as a story**
Other form: Anecdotal *(adj)*
Sentence: The book was a collection of *anecdotes* about the early settlers.

ANGUISH (ANG-wish) *noun* — **extreme mental or emotional pain; torment**
Other form: Anguished *(adj)*
Sentence: No amount of therapy could relieve the *anguish* she felt after the accident.

ANIMOSITY (anna-MAHS-ih-tee) *noun* — **ill-will; resentment; hostile feelings**
Sentence: The *animosity* between the two brothers eventually flared into violence.

ANNEX (uh-NEX) *verb* — **to add or attach a new section**
Other form: Annex *(noun);* annexation *(noun)*
Sentence: A nation will sometimes *annex* a new territory simply because it can.

ANOMALY (uh-NOM-ih-lee) *noun* — **something that deviates from what is expected**
Other form: Anomalous *(adj)*
Sentence: Among the planets, Pluto's irregular orbit is an *anomaly.*

ANONYMOUS (uh-NON-ih-mus) *adj* — **nameless; unidentified**
Other form: Anonymously *(adv)*
Sentence: She spent days trying to figure out who could have sent the *anonymous* letter.

ANTECEDENT (ANN-teh-see-dent) *noun* — **a prior event, usually with subsequent effects**
Other form: Antecedent *(adj)*
Sentence: A set of repressive laws served as an *antecedent* to the rebellion.

ANTEDILUVIAN (ann-tee-dih-LOO-vee-in) *adj* — **before the Biblical flood; very old**
Other form: Antediluvian *(noun)*
Sentence: He was branded as an *antediluvian* because of his traditional views.

ANTHOLOGY (ann-THOL-uh-jee) *noun* — **a collection of artistic pieces of the same form**
   Other form: Anthological *(adj)*
   Sentence: She was thrilled that the editor of the *anthology* wanted to include her poem.

ANTIDOTE (ANN-tih-dote) *noun* — **something that counteracts negative effects**
   Other form: Antidote *(verb)*
   Sentence: He searched frantically for the *antidote* as his poisoned friend lay dying.

ANTISEPTIC (ann-tih-SEP-tik) *adj* — **germ-free**
   Other form: Antiseptic *(noun)*
   Sentence: The instruments are scrubbed with an *antiseptic* solution before each surgery.

APHORISM (AFF-er-izm) *noun* — **a truth stated in one sentence; maxim**
   Other forms: Aphoristic *(adj)*; aphoristically *(adv)*
   Sentence: Some of the best *aphorisms* appear in fortune cookies.

APLOMB (uh-PLOM) *noun* — **self-assurance; poise**
   Sentence: The renowned cellist walked onto the stage with *aplomb*.

APOCRYPHAL (uh-PAHK-ruh-ful) *adj* — **of doubtful or unverifiable authorship**
   Other form: Apocrypha *(noun)*
   Sentence: Those writings are *apocryphal* and cannot be used as evidence.

APOSTATE (uh-PAH-state) *noun* — **person who has abandoned his religion or beliefs**
   Other form: Apostate *(adj)*
   Sentence: In certain cultures, an *apostate* has all but dropped out of society.

APOTHEOSIS (uh-PAH-thee-oh-siss) *noun* — **ultimate status; divine form**
   Other form: Apotheosize *(verb)*
   Sentence: In his eyes, she was the *apotheosis* of what a woman should be.

APPRAISE (uh-PRAZE) *verb* — **to judge the value of something; estimate**
   Other form: Appraisal *(noun)*
   Sentence: Our local antique expert *appraised* the watch at one hundred dollars.

APPREHEND (app-ree-HEND) *verb* — **to take hold of; to arrest**
  Other form: Apprehension *(noun)*
  Sentence: The bank robber was *apprehended* by the police within minutes.

APPREHENSIVE (app-ree-HEN-siv) *adj* — **feeling great anxiety; worried**
  Other form: Apprehensively *(adv)*
  Sentence: She said her son could go rock-climbing, but she was *apprehensive* about it.

APPROBATION (app-roh-BAY-shun) *noun* — **approval**
  Other form: Approbate *(verb)*
  Sentence: Surprisingly, my unusual idea was met with complete *approbation*.

APROPOS (ap-ruh-PO) *adj* — **relevant; appropriate**
  Other form: Apropos *(adv)*
  Sentence: Your serious words were *apropos*, given the grave situation we're facing.

ARABLE (AHR-uh-bull) *adj* — **soil that is suitable for crop production**
  Other form: Arability *(noun)*
  Sentence: After months without rain, all of the *arable* land had turned to desert.

ARBITER (AR-bih-ter) *noun* — **person having the authority to settle a dispute**
  Other form: Arbitrate *(verb)*
  Sentence: We couldn't come to an agreement, so we let an impartial *arbiter* decide.

ARBOREAL (ar-BOR-ee-uhl) *adj* — **relating to or resembling a tree**
  Other form: Arboreally *(adv)*
  Sentence: The *arboreal* habitats of most birds keep them safe from predators.

ARDOR (AR-der) *noun* — **heated emotion; passion**
  Sentence: She campaigned with an *ardor* unmatched by her opponents.

ARDUOUS (AR-joo-uss) *adj* — **difficult; onerous**
  Other form: Arduously *(adv)*
  Sentence: Climbing Mount Everest is an *arduous*, and dangerous, task.

ARID (ARR-id) *adj* — **excessively dry; parched**
    Other forms: Aridity *(noun);* aridly *(adv)*
    Sentence: Accustomed to the tropics, he found the *arid* climate oppressive.

ARRANT (AHR-ent) *adj* — **1. wandering 2. shameless**
    Other form: Arrantly *(adv)*
    Sentence: He was an *arrant* con artist, and difficult to catch.

ARROGATE (ARRA-gate) *verb* — **to seize a right or power that one is not entitled to**
    Other form: Arrogation *(noun)*
    Sentence: The junior executive tried to *arrogate* the authority of his boss.

ARTIFICE (ART-ih-fiss) *noun* — **something achieved through trickery or cleverness**
    Other form: Artificial *(adj)*
    Sentence: The trust he inspired in others turned out to be an *artifice*.

ASCERTAIN (ah-ser-TANE) *verb* — **to investigate and make sure of; discover**
    Other forms: Ascertainable *(adj);* ascertainment *(noun)*
    Sentence: After years of research, scientists have *ascertained* the cause of the disease.

ASCRIBE (uh-SCRIBE) *verb* — **to explain by referring to an assumed cause**
    Other forms: Ascription *(noun);* ascriptive *(adj)*
    Sentence: The conquerors *ascribed* their dominance to a moral superiority.

ASPERSION (uh-SPUR-zhun) *noun* — **negative statement about someone's character**
    Other form: Asperse *(verb)*
    Sentence: The *aspersions* against him were disproved, but the damage had been done.

ASSESS (uh-SESS) *verb* — **to analyze in order to determine merit or value**
    Other form: Assessment *(noun)*
    Sentence: A good teacher will try to *assess* the strengths and needs of each student.

ASTRINGENT (uh-STRIN-jint) *adj* — **having the ability to pucker soft tissue**
    Other form: Astringency *(noun)*
    Sentence: For most people, lemon juice has an *astringent* effect in the mouth.

ASYLUM (uh-SY-lum) *noun* — **a place of protection or refuge**
Sentence: Hounded by the noises of city life, she found *asylum* in the library.

ATONE (uh-TONE) *verb* — **to make reparations or amends for an offense**
Other form: Atonement *(noun)*
Sentence: He was ordered to *atone* for his crime by doing community service.

ATTENUATE (uh-TEN-yoo-ate) *verb* — **to make thin or weaker; to lessen**
Other form: Attenuation *(noun)*
Sentence: The heavy clouds *attenuated* the signal, making it hard to hear the pilot.

AUTONOMOUS (aw-TAHN-uh-muss) *adj* — **free; self-directing**
Other form: Autonomy *(noun)*
Sentence: The symbol of an autonomous nation is the drafting of its own constitution.

AUXILIARY (awg-ZILL-yah-ree) *adj* — **functioning in a role of assistance or support**
Other form: Auxiliary *(noun)*
Sentence: This was the first time the *auxiliary* team was needed.

AVER (uh-VER) *verb* — **to declare or verify**
Sentence: The accused took the stand and forcefully *averred* his innocence.

AVERSION (uh-VER-zhun) *noun* — **an intense dislike and a desire to avoid something**
Other form: Averse *(adj)*
Sentence: She had an *aversion* to fish, and wouldn't eat in a restaurant that served it.

AVOCATION (av-oh-KAY-shun) *noun* — **hobby**
Other form: Avocational *(adj)*
Sentence: After my workday is done, I turn to my *avocation*, which is music.

AVOW (uh-VOW) *verb* — **to state as a fact; claim; assert**
Other form: Avow *(noun)*
Sentence: We left the tiny island and *avowed* that we would never return.

BALK (BAWK) *verb* — **to refuse to move forward; to back away from a proposed idea**
    Other form: Balk *(noun)*
    Sentence: An honest congressman, he *balked* at the offer of a bribe.

BALLAD (BAL-id) *noun* — **a song that tells a story, often romantic in nature**
    Other form: Ballad *(verb)*
    Sentence: There's a *ballad* they've been singing in these mountains for centuries.

BASK (BASK) *verb* — **to expose oneself to a pleasing experience; luxuriate**
    Sentence: The returning hero *basked* in the glory of a parade given in his honor.

BEATIFY (bee-ATT-ih-fye) *verb* — **to make extremely happy; to bring bliss**
    Other forms: Beatific *(adj);* beatification *(noun)*
    Sentence: The bride appeared *beatified*, as though she had never been happier.

BEGRUDGE (be-GRUJ) *verb* — **to yield or acknowledge with hesitation; envy**
    Other form: Begrudgingly *(adv)*
    Sentence: We *begrudge* him the expensive cars, because he's never had to work.

BELABOR (bee-LAY-ber) *verb* — **to work at or dwell on too long; overdo**
    Sentence: Everyone understood, but he continued to *belabor* the point anyway.

BELLICOSE (BELL-uh-kose) *adj* — **inclined toward fighting; aggressive**
    Other forms: Bellicosely *(adv);* bellicosity *(noun)*
    Sentence: He was a *bellicose* boss and his employees feared him.

BEMOAN (be-MOAN) *verb* — **to repeatedly express grief or disappointment**
    Other form: Bemoaningly
    Sentence: Three years later, she was still *bemoaning* the loss of her cat.

BENEFACTOR (BEN-uh-fak-ter) *noun* — **a person who actively helps others**
    Other form: Benefaction *(noun)*
    Sentence: The local hospital would not exist were it not for a handful of *benefactors*.

BERATE (bee-RATE) *verb* — **criticize harshly**
Sentence: Military recruits are often *berated* by their superiors to perform better.

BEREFT (buh-REFT) *adj* — **totally deprived**
Other forms: Bereave *(verb);* bereavement *(noun)*
Sentence: She was tossed out into the street, *bereft* of her possessions and her dignity.

BESEECH (be-SEECH) *verb* — **beg; implore; plead**
Other form: Beseechingly *(adv)*
Sentence: I *beseeched* the judge for mercy, but he ignored my pleas.

BESET (be-SET) *verb* — **to trouble or attack**
Other form: Besetment *(noun)*
Sentence: Our relationship was *beset* with problems from the first day.

BEWILDER (be-WILL-der) *verb* — **to confuse or perplex**
Other form: Bewilderment *(noun)*
Sentence: Even with a map, we were completely *bewildered* by the maze of streets.

BILGE (BILJ) *noun* — **dull or worthless ideas**
Other form: Bilge *(noun)* – part of a ship that sits below the water
Sentence: His editorial was filled with *bilge* and pointless arguments.

BILK (BILK) *verb* — **to cheat or defraud**
Other form: Bilk *(noun)*
Sentence: Elderly people are often *bilked* out of their life savings.

BLANDISH (BLAN-dish) *verb* — **to coax with sweet words; to flatter**
Other forms: Blandishing *(adj)*; blandishingly *(adv)*; blandishment *(noun)*
Sentence: You can *blandish* me all you want, but I'm not giving in.

BLATANT (BLAY-tent) *adj* — **obvious in a vulgar manner; brazen; loud**
Other forms: Blatancy *(noun);* blatantly *(adv)*
Sentence: Employees were *blatantly* stealing, often right in front of the manager.

BLEMISH (BLEM-ish) *noun* — **a physical or moral flaw**
Other form: Blemish *(verb)*
Sentence: A speeding ticket was the only *blemish* in her otherwise perfect driving record.

BLITHE (BLYTH) *adj* — **cheerful; carefree**
Other form: Blithely *(adv)*
Sentence: He was a *blithe* spirit, seemingly without a worry in the world.

BOISTEROUS (BOYCE-ter-uss) *adj* — **aggressively loud; rowdy; clamorous**
Other forms: Boisterously *(adv);* boisterousness *(noun)*
Sentence: After a few drinks, some people became *boisterous* and even violent.

BOORISH (BOOR-ish) *adj* — **lacking in social skills; rude; unmannered**
Other forms: Boor *(noun);* boorishness *(noun)*
Sentence: No one understood why this *boor* had been invited to such an elegant party.

BOURGEOIS (burzh-WAH) *noun* — **person or class of people strongly focused on profit**
Other form: Bourgeois *(adj)*
Sentence: When he returned to his poor village, his new *bourgeois* ways aroused distrust.

BRAZEN (BRAY-zuhn) *adj* — **lacking delicacy or sensitivity; shameless**
Other forms: Brazenly *(adv); brazenness (noun)*
Sentence: She flirted *brazenly* with every married man in the town.

BREACH (BREECH) *verb* — **to break or violate a physical defense or an oath or law**
Other form: Breach *(noun)*
Sentence: They were sued by the company for *breach* of contract.

BRITTLE (BRIT-til) *adj* — **easily broken or cracked; fragile**
Other form: Brittleness *(noun)*
Sentence: The frigid air made the tree limbs *brittle*, and they snapped off in the wind.

BROACH (BROACH) *verb* — **to introduce, announce, or present**
Other form: Broach *(noun)*
Sentence: We finally worked up the courage to *broach* the subject.

BRUSQUE (BRUSK) *adj* — **abrupt and without gentleness**
  Other forms: Brusquely *(adv);* brusqueness *(noun)*
  Sentence: His short answers and *brusque* manner made everyone uncomfortable.

BUFFET (BUFF-it) *verb* — **to hit repeatedly and rhythmically**
  Other form: Buffet (buff-AY *(noun)* – meal at which diners serve themselves
  Sentence: The wind nearly *buffeted* the small plane right into the sea.

BULWARK (BULL-wark) *noun* — **that which provides support or protection**
  Other form: Bulwark *(verb)*
  Sentence: His assistant was a *bulwark* of strength throughout the ordeal.

BUOYANT (BOY-ent) *adj* — **having the ability to soar or float**
  Other forms: Buoyancy *(noun);* buoyantly *(adv)*
  Sentence: We were in a *buoyant* mood after hearing the good news.

BURGEON (BURR-jin) *verb* — **to grow quickly and in all directions; swell; flourish**
  Sentence: The *burgeoning* business created jobs and attracted people to the city.

BURNISH (BURR-nish) *verb* — **to rub in order to make shiny or smooth; polish**
  Other forms: Burnished *(adj);* burnisher *(noun)*
  Sentence: The *burnished* bronze sculpture shone in the sunlight.

BUTTRESS (BUH-tress) *verb* — **to support or strengthen**
  Other form: Buttress *(noun)*
  Sentence: The attorney *buttressed* her arguments with solid evidence.

CABAL (ka-BAHL) *noun* — **group of people plotting to overthrow an authority figure**
  Sentence: Members of the *cabal* were arrested before they could carry out their plan.

CADENCE (KAY-dents) *noun* — **the rhythmic flow of a spoken language**
  Other form: Cadent *(adj)*
  Sentence: He claimed to be from Egypt, but his speech did not have the right *cadence*.

CADGE (CAJ) *verb* — **to habitually beg**
    Other form: Cadger *(noun)*
    Sentence: His skill at *cadging* left him no motivation to work for a living.

CALLOUS (KAL-uss) *adj* — **emotionally detached; insensitive**
    Other form: Callousness *(noun)*
    Sentence: He developed a *callous* facade to protect himself from emotional pain.

CALLOW (KAL-oh) *adj* — **lacking adult sophistication; immature**
    Other form: Callowness *(noun)*
    Sentence: We expected a worldly adult, but found a *callow* child.

CALUMNY (KAL-um-nee) *noun* — **false statements meant to harm another's reputation**
    Other form: Calumnious *(adj)*
    Sentence: The essay was filled with *calumny* and slander.

CAMARADERIE (kam-uh-RAH-der-ee) *noun* — **good will among friends; fellowship**
    Sentence: We always look forward to the *camaraderie* of the camping trip.

CANNY (KAN-ee) *adj* — **wise; foresighted; prudent**
    Other forms: Cannily *(adv);* canniness *(noun)*
    Sentence: Arctic explorers had to be *canny*, or they didn't make it back alive.

CANT (KANT) *adj* — **the repetitive or insincere use of religious statements**
    Sentence: The sermon was a disappointing mixture of *cant* and cliches.

CANTANKEROUS (kan-TANK-er-uss) *adj* — **irritable; cranky; contrary**
    Other forms: Cantankerously *(adv);* cantankerousness *(noun)*
    Sentence: The landlord was *cantankerous*, so we tried to stay on his good side.

CAPTIVATE (KAP-tih-vate) *verb* — **to influence with charm or charisma**
    Other forms: Captivating *(adj);* captivation *(noun)*
    Sentence: Everyone in the audience was *captivated* by the young girl's enthusiasm.

CARICATURE (KAR-ih-kah-choor) *noun* — **a satiric representation using exaggeration**
Other form: Caricature *(verb)*
Sentence: An artist at the carnival drew my *caricature* in less than a minute.

CAROUSE (kuh-ROWZ) *verb* — **to drink excessively, usually in a group**
Other form: Carousal *(noun)*
Sentence: The rumor was that he spent several nights a week *carousing* with his buddies.

CAUCUS (KAW-kuss) *noun* — **a meeting to decide policy, candidates, or delegates**
Other form: Caucus *(verb)*
Sentence: Anticipating a close election, caucus *members* turned out in record numbers.

CAVORT (kuv-VORT) *verb* — **to dance around in some delightful activity**
Sentence: The way he was *cavorting* around, he sure didn't seem depressed to me.

CENTURION (sen-TOOR-ec-uhn) *noun* — **a Roman officer commanding a hundred men**
Sentence: In the effort to expand the empire, Rome's *centurions* were willing to die.

CEREBRAL (suh-REE-bruhl) *adj* — **having to do with the use of the mind; intellectual**
Other form: Cerebrally *(adv)*
Sentence: The play was very *cerebral*, and the lack of action made it dull to watch.

CHAOS (KAY-oss) *noun* — **an unorganized state; total confusion**
Other form: Chaotic *(adj)*
Sentence: For some reason, this practical woman enjoyed the *chaos* of the classroom.

CHARY (CHAR-ee) *adj* — **extremely cautious; hesitant**
Other form: Charily *(adv)*
Sentence: He had lost money in the stock market and was *chary* of investing again.

CHAUVINIST (SHO-vin-ist) *noun* — **one who is blindly loyal to a person or group**
Other forms: Chauvinism *(noun)*; chauvinistic *(adj); chauvinistically (adv)*
Sentence: A *chauvinist* attitude prevents him from really thinking for himself.

CHICANERY (shi-KANE-er-ee) *noun* — **trickery; deception**
Other form: Chicane *(verb)*
Sentence: The son of two con artists, he was raised on *chicanery* and lies.

CHOLERIC (kuh-LERR-ik) *adj* — **easily angered; hot-tempered**
Other forms: Choler *(noun);* cholerically *(adv)*
Sentence: He seemed mild-mannered, so we were surprised by his *choleric* outbursts.

CIRCUITOUS (sir-KYOO-ih-tuss) *adj* — **following a circular course**
Other forms: Circuitously *(adv);* circuitousness *(noun)*
Sentence: Her *circuitous* logic left us all confused.

CIRCUMLOCUTION (sir-kum-lo-KYOO-shun) *noun* — **vague and wordy speech that intentionally avoids a topic or answer**
Other form: Circumlocutory *(adj)*
Sentence: A master of *circumlocution*, the mayor replied at length, and said nothing.

CIRCUMVENT (sir-kum-VENT) *verb* — **to shrewdly avoid effects or requirements**
Other form: Circumvention *(noun)*
Sentence: As a visiting diplomat, he was able to *circumvent* the law and go unpunished.

CITADEL (SIT-uh-dell) *noun* — **fortress; stronghold**
Sentence: The *citadel* stood on the town's highest hill, and was never attacked.

CLAIRVOYANT (klare-VOY-ent) *adj* — **supposed ability to see from a great distance**
Other forms: Clairvoyance; clairvoyant *(nouns)*
Sentence: Mothers are *clairvoyant*, and know what their kids are doing in another room.

CLAMOR (KLAMM-er) *noun* — **a loud confusion of noise, especially voices**
Other forms: Clamor *(verb)*; clamorous *(adj);* clamorousness *(noun)*
Sentence: It was difficult to hear each other above the *clamor* of the crowd.

CLANDESTINE (klan-DEST-in) *adj* — **conducted in secrecy**
Other form: Clandestinely *(adv)*
Sentence: The barking dog doomed our *clandestine* mission to failure.

COAGULATE (ko-AGG-yoo-late) *verb* — **to collect into a thicker, jellylike state**
Other forms: Coagulated *(adj)*; coagulation *(noun)*
Sentence: The liquid had *coagulated* and was impossible to pour.

CODDLE (KODD-il) *verb* — **treat with excessive care; overindulge; pamper**
Other form: Coddled *(adj)*
Sentence: His mother had *coddled* him for so long, he was helpless on his own.

COEVAL (ko-EE-vul) *adj* — **of the same age**
Other form: Coeval *(noun)*
Sentence: Those trees are thousands of years old, some *coeval* with Egypt's pyramids.

COGENT (KO-jent) *adj* — **pertinent and valid; concisely correct**
Other forms: Cogency *(noun)*; cogently *(adv)*
Sentence: The defense attorney's *cogent* final argument swayed the jury.

COGNATE (KOG-nayt) *adj* — **part of the same family; related by blood**
Other forms: Cognatic *(adj)*; cognate *(noun)*
Sentence: The monarchies of several European nations were *cognate* to each other.

COGNIZANT (KOG-nih-zent) *adj* — **having knowledge of; aware; conscious**
Other form: Cognizance *(noun)*
Sentence: We were *cognizant* of his shady past, but decided to hire him anyway.

COHERENT (ko-HEER-ent) *verb* — **logical and consistent; readily understood**
Other forms: Cohere *(verb)*; coherence *(noun)*; coherently *(adv)*
Sentence: Socrates was a master of *coherent* argument, building his ideas logically.

COLLABORATE (kuh-LABB-er-ate) *verb* — **to work together**
Other forms: Collaboratively *(adv)*; collaboration *(noun)*
Sentence: Each person had strong ideas, so it was difficult to *collaborate*.

COLLOQUIAL (kuh-LOKE-wee-uhl) *adj* — **informal speech common to a certain region**
Other form: Colloquialism *(noun)*
Sentence: Her colloquialisms were foreign to us, and we were afraid we'd misunderstand.

COLLUSION (kuh-LOO-zhun) *noun* — **a secret agreement that is illegal in nature**
Other forms: Collusive, collusory *(adv)*
Sentence: The utilities agreed to raise prices, but were charged with *collusion*.

COLOSSUS (kuh-LAHSS-iss) *noun* — **an object that is much larger than average**
Other form: Colossal *(adj)*
Sentence: Looking like a *colossus*, the ocean liner cruised past the sailboat.

COMBUSTION (kum-BUS-chun) *noun* — **a process involving the release of heat energy**
Other forms: Combust *(verb)*; combustible *(adj)*
Sentence: The internal *combustion* engine changed the way we travel.

COMMEMORATE (kuh-MEM-er-ate) *verb* — **to celebrate something from the past**
Other forms: Commemoration *(noun)*; commemorative *(adj)*
Sentence: A coin was issued to commemorate those who died in the battle.

COMMODIOUS (kuh-MODE-ee-uss) *adj* — **having ample space; roomy**
Other forms: Commodiously *(adv)*; commodiousness *(noun)*
Sentence: The compact car was surprisingly *commodious* inside.

COMPENSATE (KAHM-pen-sate) *verb* — **repay; remunerate**
Other forms: Compensable *(adj)*; compensation *(noun)*
Sentence: They tried to *compensate* us for our losses, but money was not the issue.

COMPLEMENT (KOMP-lih-ment) *verb* — **to add the missing parts; to complete**
Other forms: Complement *(noun)*; complementary *(adj)*
Sentence: On a successful team, the members *complement* each others' strengths.

COMPLIMENT (KOMP-lih-ment) *verb* — **to express admiration**
Other forms: Compliment *(noun)*; complimentary *(adj)*
Sentence: Sometimes a *compliment* is all an employee needs to stay motivated.

COMPREHENSIVE (komp-ree-HEN-siv) *adj* — **covering the full range of possibilities**
Other form: Comprehensively *(adv)*
Sentence: The textbook was so *comprehensive* that no additional reading was necessary.

COMPRESS (kum-PRESS) *verb* — **to press together into a smaller space; to squeeze**
Other forms: Compression *(noun);* compressive *(adj)*
Sentence: Somehow she *compressed* a two-hour speech into thirty minutes.

COMPUNCTION (kum-PUNK-shun) *noun* — **regret; remorse; guilt**
Other form: Compunctious *(adj)*
Sentence: Didn't you feel any *compunction* about abandoning us?

CONCEIT (kun-SEET) *noun* — **any idea, but especially an inflated self-esteem**
Other form: Conceited *(adj)*
Sentence: His own *conceit* fooled him into thinking he could meet the goal.

CONCILIATORY (kun-SILL-ee-uh-tor-ee) *adj* — **in a manner that tries to make peace; mollifying**
Other form: Conciliate *(verb)*
Sentence: Though mean-spirited during the campaign, he was *conciliatory* in defeat.

CONCOCT (kun-KOKT) *verb* — **to put together from separate materials; compose**
Other form: Concoction *(noun)*
Sentence: She *concocted* a wild theory from a handful of unrelated facts.

CONCORD (KAHN-kord) *noun* — **agreement; harmony**
Other forms: Concord *(verb);* concordant *(adj);* concordantly *(adv)*
Sentence: The holidays gave us a brief period of *concord* and good will.

CONDENSE (kun-DENSE) *verb* — **to remove unneeded parts; compress**
Other forms: Condensation *(noun);* condensed *(adj)*
Sentence: The *condensed* version was no easier to understand, but at least it was shorter.

CONDESCEND (kahn-duh-SEND) *verb* — **to lower oneself; to act superior**
Other forms: Condescendingly *(adv);* condescension *(noun)*
Sentence: His tone was *condescending* and rude.

CONDOLENCE (kun-DOE-lents) *noun* — **expression of sorrow or sympathy**
Other forms: Condole *(verb);* condolent *(adj)*
Sentence: We expressed our *condolences* in a note to the widow.

CONDUCE (kun-DOOSE) *verb* — **to promote or contribute**
Other forms: Conducive *(adj);* conduciveness *(noun)*
Sentence: Mental stamina, as well as strong legs and lungs, *conduce* to successful running.

CONDUIT (KAHN-doo-it) *noun* — **that which allows something to flow from here to there**
Sentence: The farmers built a *conduit* to carry water to their dry fields.

CONFIDANT (KAHN-fih-dant) *noun* — **a person entrusted with secrets**
Other form: Confide *(verb)*; confidante *(female)*
Sentence: In prison, cellmates frequently become each other's *confidant*.

CONFLAGRATION (kahn-fluh-GRAY-shun) *noun* — **large, spreading fire**
Other forms: Conflagrant *(adj);* conflagrate *(verb)*
Sentence: A tiny spark quickly became a *conflagration* in the dry forest.

CONFLUENCE (KAHN-floo-ense) *noun* — **meeting place; point of joining**
Other form: Confluent *(adj)*
Sentence: Towns often sprang up at the *confluence* of two rivers.

CONFORMIST (kun-FORM-ist) *noun* — **person who follows or obeys a set of rules**
Other forms: Conform *(verb);* conformity *(noun)*
Sentence: I grew tired of rebelling and became a *conformist*.

CONGEAL (kun-JEEL) *verb* — **to turn from liquid to a semi-solid; coagulate**
Other form: Congealment *(noun)*
Sentence: The soup had *congealed* into an inedible mass.

CONGENIAL (kun-JEEN-ee-uhl) *adj* — **having the same nature; compatible**
Other form: Congeniality *(noun)*
Sentence: On vacation, there is often a *congenial* mood, even among strangers.

CONGENITAL (kun-JEN-ih-tull) *adj* — **pertaining to a trait acquired during development**
Other form: Congenitally *(adv)*
Sentence: Her small stature is a *congenital* condition; her parents are both normal height.

CONGREGATION (kahn-grah-GAY-shun) *noun* — **gathering of people for a common purpose; assembly**
Other form: Congregate *(verb)*
Sentence: The religious leader inspired the *congregation* with his words.

CONJECTURE (kun-JEK-shur) *noun* — **a reasonable guess, but still based on little fact**
Other form: Conjecture *(verb)*
Sentence: Astronomers had *conjectured* the existence of Pluto long before it was found.

CONJOIN (kun-JOYN) *verb* — **bring together for a shared purpose; unite**
Other forms: Conjoined *(adj);* conjointment *(noun)*
Sentence: They *conjoined* their interests toward a common goal.

CONNIVE (kah-NIVE) *verb* — **to pretend ignorance of wrongdoing; to conspire**
Other form: Connivance *(noun)*
Sentence: We assume a certain amount of *conniving* is necessary in politics.

CONNOISSEUR (kahn-uh-soor) *noun* — **one who combines expert knowledge and enjoyment of something**
Sentence: My sister is a *connoisseur* of 18th Century fiction.

CONNOTATION (kahn-oh-TAY-shun) *noun* — **an implied or secondary meaning**
Other forms: Connotative *(adj)* connote *(verb)*
Sentence: His words had strong *connotations* for a variety of people, in a variety of ways.

CONSECRATE (KAHN-suh-krate) *verb* — **to declare something sacred**
Other form: Consecration *(noun)*
Sentence: The former site of the temple was *consecrated* and considered holy.

CONSENSUS (kun-SEN-sus) *adj* — **agreement among a group; unanimity; accord**
Sentence: We'd expected disagreement, but there was a *consensus* on the first vote.

CONSIGN (kun-SINE) *verb* — **to entrust to someone else**
Other form: Consignment *(noun)*
Sentence: Before entering the hospital, he *consigned* his possessions to his friend.

CONSOLE (kun-SOLE) *verb* — **to help soothe someone in pain or grief**
Other forms: Consolation *(noun);* consolatory *(adj)*
Sentence: Though surrounded by family, the man could not be *consoled.*

CONSPICUOUS (kun-SPIK-yoo-uss) *adj* — **easily noticed; obvious**
Other forms: Conspicuously *(adv);* conspicuousness *(noun)*
Sentence: The more we tried to blend into the crowd, the more *conspicuous* we felt.

CONSTERNATION (kahn-stir-NAY-shun) *noun* — **a state of confused distress**
Other form: Consternate *(verb)*
Sentence: His first night in prison was a mixture of *consternation* and fear.

CONSTITUENT (kun-STIH-choo-ent) *noun* — **an essential component; element**
Other form: Constituent *(adj)*
Sentence: We now know that atoms have much smaller *constituent* particles.

CONSTRAIN (kun-STRANE) *verb* — **to restrict; to stifle**
Other form: Constraint *(noun)*
Sentence: The artist felt her creativity was *constrained* by the many rules and limitations.

CONSTRICT (kun-STRIKT) *verb* — **to squeeze; to compress**
Other forms: Constricted *(adj)*; constriction *(noun)*
Sentence: She could feel her throat *constricting*, an allergic reaction to the food.

CONSTRUE (kun-STROO) *verb* — **to understand in a particular way**
Sentence: I *construed* his words to mean that we should proceed.

CONTEMPORANEOUS (kun-tem-por-AY-nee-uss) *adj* — **at the same time; coincident**
Other forms: Contemporaneously *(adv);* contemporaneousness *(noun)*
Sentence: The rise of Nazism in Germany was *contemporaneous* with Fascism in Italy.

CONTENTIOUS (kun-TENT-shuss) *adj* — **prone to arguments or fights; belligerent**
Other forms: Contentiously *(adv);* contentiousness *(noun)*
Sentence: His *contentious* nature made it difficult to have a pleasant discussion.

CONTIGUOUS (kun-TIG-yoo-uss) *adj* — **sharing boundaries; bordering; adjacent**
  Other forms: Contiguously *(adv);* contiguity *(noun)*
  Sentence: The United States and Canada are *contiguous* for thousands of miles.

CONTRAVENE (kahn-trah-VEEN) *verb* — **to interfere, obstruct, or oppose**
  Other form: Contravention *(noun)*
  Sentence: We wanted to *contravene* her decision to move away, but she was determined.

CONTRIVED (kun-TRIVED) *adj* — **designed; invented; put together**
  Other forms: Contrive *(verb);* contrivance *(noun)*
  Sentence: He *contrived* the entire plan by himself, in his head, while showering.

CONTUMACIOUS (kahn-too-MAY-shuss) *adj* — **defiant; insubordinate**
  Other forms: Contumaciously *(adv);* contumacy *(noun)*
  Sentence: Her *contumacious* attitude toward authority made her unfit for the military.

CONTUSION (kun-TOO-zhun) *noun* — **a bruise or wound**
  Other form: Contuse *(verb)*
  Sentence: Though struck by the car, he was treated for minor *contusions* and released.

CONVALESCENCE (kahn-vuh-LESS) *noun* — **gradual recovery from injury or illness**
  Other forms: Convalesce *(verb);* convalescent *(adj)*
  Sentence: My *convalescence* was helped by the mild climate and soothing quiet.

CONVENE (kun-VEEN) *verb* — **to assemble or congregate for a specific purpose**
  Other forms: Convenable *(adj);* convention *(noun)*
  Sentence: We *convened* at one and by two-thirty were on our way home.

CONVOLUTED (kahn-vuh-LOOT-ed) *adj* — **complicated; twisted; coiled**
  Other forms: Convolute *(verb);* convolution *(noun)*
  Sentence: The story told by the witness was so *convoluted*, the jury couldn't follow it.

CORNUCOPIA (kor-nah-KO-pee-uh) *noun* — **an abundance of good things**
  Other form: Cornucopian *(adj)*
  Sentence: The store was a *cornucopia* of handmade items.

COROLLARY (KOR-uh-lerr-ee) *noun* — **an idea that follows directly from another**
Other form: Corollary *(adj)*
Sentence: Many theorems in geometry have *corollaries* that are self-evident.

CORONATION (kor-uh-NAY-shun) *noun* — **ceremony in which a person is crowned; ascension to the throne or other lofty position**
Other form: Coronate *(verb)*
Sentence: The new queen was adored, and her *coronation* a nationwide celebration.

CORPULENT (KORP-yoo-lent) *adj* — **having a large body; massive**
Other form: Corpulence *(noun)*
Sentence: Sumo wrestlers must be *corpulent* and agile.

CORRELATE (KORA-late) *verb* — **to have or demonstrate a strong connection**
Other forms: Correlated *(adj)*; correlation *(noun)*
Sentence: One could *correlate* the temperature of the water with the condition of the fish.

CORROBORATION (kuh-rah-ber-AY-shun) *noun* —**confirmation of a previous statement**
Other form: Corroborate *(verb)*; corroborative *(adj)*
Sentence: The second witness provided solid *corroboration* of yesterday's testimony.

COSMOPOLITAN (koz-muh-PAHL-uh-tin) *adj* — **worldly; experience; sophisticated**
Other form: Cosmopolitan *(noun)*
Sentence: She was *cosmopolitan* and he had never been off the family farm.

COUNTENANCE (KOWN-ten-ance) *noun* — **facial expression**
Other form: Countenance *(verb)* – to approve of; sanction
Sentence: He claimed to be happy, but his gloomy *countenance* said otherwise.

COUNTERFEIT (KOWN-ter-fit) *adj* — **fake but intended to look real in order to fool**
Other forms: Counterfeit, counterfeiter *(noun)*
Sentence: Even the art expert had been fooled by the *counterfeit* painting.

COUNTERVAIL (kown-ter-VALE) *verb* — **to oppose with nearly equal force; counteract**
Other form: Countervailing *(adj)*
Sentence: The two *countervailing* storms negated each other, and we had calm weather.

COVERT (ko-VERT) *adj* — **hidden; concealed; done in a secret manner**
Other forms: Covertly *(adv);* covertness *(noun)*
Sentence: Once the *covert* mission was discovered, its story appeared in every newspaper.

COVET (KUH-vet) *verb* — **to secretly wish for, especially another's possessions**
Other forms: Covetous *(adj);* covetousness *(noun)*
Sentence: Living in poverty, he *coveted* his brother's wealthy lifestyle.

COWER (KOW-er) *verb* — **to shrink away in fear; cringe**
Other form: Cowering *(adj)*
Sentence: The dog *cowered* under the desk, sure it was about to be punished.

CRASS (KRASS) *adj* — **lacking refinement or delicacy; boorish**
Other forms: Crassly *(adv);* crassness *(noun)*
Sentence: In film, a *crass* person may seem amusing; in real life, not so amusing.

CRAVEN (KRAY-ven) *adj* — **lacking any courage; cowardly**
Other forms: Cravenly *(adv);* cravenness *(noun)*
Sentence: Your attempt to blame this on others is a *craven* and irresponsible act.

CREDULITY (kra-DOOL-ih-tee) *noun* — **willingness to believe with little or no evidence**
Sentence: A magician takes advantage of the audience's *credulity*.

CREDULOUS (KREH-joo-luss) *adj* — **eagerly believing, even without solid facts**
Other forms: Credulously *(adv);* credulousness *(noun)*
Sentence: Many people are *credulous* about UFOs, even though there is little evidence.

CULMINATE (KUL-min-ayt) *verb* — **to reach a highest or climactic point**
Other form: Culmination *(noun)*
Sentence: The celebration will *culminate* with a parade and fireworks.

CURT (KERT) *adj* — **giving short, abrupt replies; terse; brusque**
Other forms: Curtly *(adv);* curtness *(noun)*
Sentence: Her answers were *curt* and evasive, and I knew something was wrong.

CURTAIL (ker-TALE) *verb* — **to shorten; cut off; diminish**
 Other forms: Curtailing *(adj)*; curtailment *(noun)*
 Sentence: He abruptly got up and left, *curtailing* any further discussion.

DEARTH (DERTH) *noun* — **a complete lack; deficiency**
 Sentence: The nation had a *dearth* of natural resources, and had to import everything.

DEBACLE (deh-BAH-kel) *noun* — **sudden breakdown; collapse; disaster**
 Sentence: What began as a calm meeting of opponents quickly became a *debacle*.

DEBASE (de-BASE) *verb* — **to lower in value; to put down; degrade**
 Other forms: Debasement *(noun)*; debasingly *(adv)*
 Sentence: He left the job feeling *debased* and unappreciated.

DEBONAIR (deb-uh-NAIR) *adj* — **graceful; charming; lighthearted**
 Other forms: Debonairly *(adv)*; debonairness *(noun)*
 Sentence: The rude and awkward boy had somehow matured into a *debonair* man.

DECIMATE (DESS-ih-mayt) *verb* — **to destroy almost completely**
 Other form: Decimation *(noun)*
 Sentence: The earthquake had *decimated* the town, leaving few structures standing.

DECOROUS (deh-KOR-uss) *adj* — **decent; proper; well-behaved**
 Other forms: Decorously (adv); decorum *(noun)*
 Sentence: The thief's *decorous* manner gave no hint of the criminal mind at work.

DECORUM (deh-KOR-um) *noun* —**proper and expected behavior**
 Other form: Decorous *(adj)*
 Sentence: He maintained his sense of *decorum* throughout the difficult ordeal.

DECRY (deh-KRY) *verb* — **to express strong disapproval; to denounce**
 Sentence: As a candidate, he *decried* the very policy he had supported all along.

DEFACE (deh-FACE) *verb* — **to destroy, mar, or injure**
    Other form: Defacement *(noun)*
    Sentence: He had *defaced* the city's most beloved statue, and was fined heavily.

DEFER (deh-FER) *verb* — **to yield to another's authority; also, postpone**
    Other forms: Deferential *(adj)*; deference *(noun)*
    Sentence: I knew the answer, but *deferred* to my boss out of respect.

DEFUNCT (deh-FUNKT) *adj* — **broken beyond repair; no longer useful; dead**
    Sentence: The once thriving business was now *defunct*, the building in shambles.

DELETERIOUS (deh-leh-TEER-ee-uss) *adj* — **harmful; destructive**
    Other forms: Deleteriously *(adv)*; deleteriousness *(noun)*
    Sentence: Almost everyone agrees that cigarettes are *deleterious* to your health.

DELINEATE (duh-LIN-ee-ate) *verb* — **to illustrate or describe in detail; outline**
    Other form: Delineation *(noun)*
    Sentence: He *delineated* his plan for the company's long-term future.

DELUDE (duh-LOOD) *verb* — **to deceive, trick, or fool**
    Other forms: Deluded *(adj)*; delusion *(noun)*
    Sentence: She had *deluded* herself into believing her husband was coming back.

DELUGE (DELL-yooj) *noun* — **an overwhelming flood**
    Other form: Deluge *(verb)*
    Sentence: His comments on the radio produced a *deluge* of angry calls.

DEMAGOGUE (DEM-uh-gog) *noun* — **someone who insincerely appeals to the wishes of the masses**
    Other form: Demagogical *(adj)*
    Sentence: Dictators offer first appear in the guise of *demagogues*.

DEMUR (dih-MUR) *verb* — **to hesitate or refuse to go along with; protest**
    Other form: Demurral *(noun)*
    Sentence: I was tempted to join in, but in the end I had to *demur*.

DENIGRATE (DEN-uh-grate) *verb* — **to say negative things about someone; defame**
Other forms: Denigration *(noun);* denigratory *(adj)*
Sentence: It was hard to listen to him *denigrate* someone he once loved.

DENIZEN (DEN-uh-zin) *noun* — **an inhabitant of a particular place**
Sentence: All *denizens* of the desert must find ways to keep cool.

DENOUEMENT (DAY-noo-mwa) *noun* — **final result of a long series of events**
Sentence: The husband and wife fought for two years to the *denouement* of divorce.

DEPOSITION (dep-uh-ZIH-shun) *noun* — **a statement or testimony that is written down; also, the removal of a monarch from the throne**
Other form: Depose *(verb)*
Sentence: The lawyer needed her *deposition* in order to proceed with the trial.

DEPRAVE (deh-PRAVE) *verb* — **to make bad; to corrupt**
Other forms: Depraved *(adj)*; depravity *(noun)*
Sentence: Spending time with crimnals can *deprave* your sense of right and wrong.

DEPRAVITY (deh-PRAV-ih-tee) *noun* — **a state of sinfulness or immorality**
Other forms: Deprave *(verb)*; depraved *(adj)*
Sentence: He had sunk to a level of *depravity* unexpected by the other gang members.

DERELICT (DERR-uh-likt) *adj* — **lacking in responsibility; neglectful**
Other form: Derelict *(noun)*
Sentence: The officer was deemed *derelict* in his duties and removed from his post.

DERISION (deh-RIH-zhun) *noun* — **the expression of ridicule or contempt**
Other forms: Deride *(verb)*; derisive *(adj)*; derisively *(adv)*
Sentence: He quit the team, unable to stand the constant *derision* from the other players.

DERIVATIVE (duh-RIV-uh-tiv) *adj* — **having developed from something else**
Other forms: Derivation *(noun)*; derivational *(adj)*; derive *(verb)*
Sentence: Each of these legends seems to be *derivative* of an earlier story.

DEROGATORY (duh-ROG-uh-tor-ee) *adj* — **expressing a bad opinion; disdainful**
Other forms: Derogative *(adj)*; derogate *(verb)*
Sentence: Rather than focusing on issues, many candidates resort to *derogatory* remarks.

DESCRY (dess-KRY) *verb* — **to see or discover after careful examination**
Sentence: We spent hours peering through the telescope, but couldn't *descry* the comet.

DESECRATE (DESS-ih-krate) *verb* — **violate the sanctity of a revered object or place**
Other form: Desecration *(noun)*
Sentence: The shrine had been *desecrated* with graffiti and litter.

DESICCANT (DESS-uh-kint) *noun* — **an agent used for drying**
Other forms: Desiccate *(verb)*; desiccated *(adv)*; desiccation *(noun)*
Sentence: The ancient Egyptians discovered the best *desiccants* for mummifying bodies.

DETER (dee-TER) *verb* — **discourage; dissuade; inhibit**
Other forms: Deterrent *(adv)*; deterrence *(noun)*
Sentence: The possibility of imprisonment helps *deter* people from committing crimes.

DETRACTION (de-TRAK-shun) *noun* — **speech designed to promote negativity; slander**
Other forms: Detract *(verb)*; detractive *(adj)*
Sentence: His comments were meant as a *detraction*, and they found their target.

DEVIOUS (DEEV-ee-uss) *adj* — **straying from the expected path; tricky; sneaky**
Other forms: Deviously *(adv)*; deviousness *(noun)*
Sentence: It's hard to predict the actions of such a *devious* person.

DIALECT (DYE-uh-lekt) *noun* — **a variation of a language, usually caused by the geographical isolation of a group**
Sentence: My grandmother could speak both formal Italian and a *dialect*.

DIAPHANOUS (dye-AFF-uh-nuss) *adj* — **clear; transparent; sheer**
Other forms: Diaphanously *(adv)*; diaphanousness *(noun)*
Sentence: The butterfly's wings were *diaphanous* and delicate.

DIDACTIC (dye-DAK-tic) *adj* — **overly concerned with teaching a lesson**
Other form: Didacticism *(noun)* Sentence: His lectures were dry, *didactic*, and dull.

DIFFIDENT (DIFF-ih-dent) *adj* — **lacking confidence; timid**

Other forms: Diffidence *(noun)*; diffidently *(adv)*
Sentence: Smart and talented, his *diffidence* is all that held him back.

DILATE (DYE-late) *verb* — **to expand; swell; widen**
Other forms: Dilated *(adj)*; dilation *(noun)*
Sentence: Her pupils were fully *dilated* and did not respond to light.

DILETTANTE (DILL-uh-tant) *noun* — **one who dabbles in an art form or field of study**
Other form: Dilettante *(adj)*
Sentence: She wanted us to think of her as a connoisseur, but she was more of a *dilettante*.

DILIGENT (DILL-uh-jent) *adj* — **hard-working and attentive to detail; industrious**
Other forms: Diligence *(noun)*; diligently *(adv)*
Sentence: A *diligent* student will often do better than one with more innate intelligence.

DIMINUTIVE (dih-MIN-yoo-tiv) *adj* — **small in size**
Other forms: Diminution, diminutive *(nouns)*; diminutively *(adv)*
Sentence: Our *diminutive* neighbor instilled fear in men twice her size.

DISALLOW (diss-uh-LOW) *verb* — **refuse to accept or even consider; reject**
Other form: Disallowance *(noun)*
Sentence: The judge *disallowed* the new evidence because of technical reasons.

DISAVOW (diss-uh-VOW) *verb* — **refuse to acknowledge; deny**
Other form: Disavowal *(noun)*
Sentence: The accused conspirator *disavowed* any knowledge of the plot.

DISCOMFIT (diss-KUM-fit) *verb* — **to upset or embarrass**
Other form: Discomfit *(noun)*
Sentence: She was so *discomfited* by the topic that she couldn't speak.

DISCOUNTENANCE (diss-KOWN-ten-ents) *noun* — **dispproval; discouragement**
Other form: Discount *(verb); discountable (adj)*
Sentence: Their *discountenance* of our idea was expected; they never listen to us.

DISCREDIT (diss-KRED-it) *verb* — **to lower in public opinion; disgrace**
Other form: Discredited *(adj)*
Sentence: A public figure can be permanently *discredited* because of a single remark.

DISCREET (diss-KREET) *adj* — **tactful; careful; modest**
Other forms: Discreetly (adv); discretion *(noun)*
Sentence: The situation is embarrassing, so let's try to be *discreet* in our questioning.

DISCREPANCY (diss-KREP-en-see) *noun* — **inconsistency; contradiction**
Other forms: Discrepant *(adj);* discrepantly *(adv)*
Sentence: There was a glaring *discrepancy* in his two versions of the story.

DISCRETE (diss-KREET) *adj* — **having a quality of separateness or individuality**
Other form: Discreteness *(noun)*
Sentence: In a cake, the *discrete* ingredients become blended and part of the whole.

DISCRIMINATE (diss-KRIM-ih-nate) *verb* — **to distinguish the differences in a group**
Other forms: Discriminating *(adj);* discrimination *(noun)*
Sentence: We're not experts, and couldn't *discriminate* between the two wines.

DISCURSIVE (diss-KUR-siv) *adj* — **jumping around unpredictably; roaming**
Other forms: Discursively *(adv);* discursiveness *(noun)*
Sentence: The speech began *logically*, but soon became discursive and hard to follow.

DISINGENUOUS (diss-in-JEN-yoo-us) *adj* — **shrewd; sneaky; insincere**
Other forms: Disingenuously *(adv);* disingenuousness *(noun)*
Sentence: I wanted to trust him, but he came across as *disingenuous* and deceitful.

DISINTERESTED (diss-IN-tuh-ress-ted) *adj* — **objective; impartial; unbiased**
Other forms: Disinterest *(noun);* disinterestedly *(adv)*
Sentence: We were all too emotional and needed a *disinterested* party to help us decide.

DISPARITY (diss-PAIR-ih-tee) *noun* — **difference; inequality**
  Other form: Disparate *(adj)*
  Sentence: There was a definite *disparity* between the service at the two restaurants.

DISPEL (dih-SPELL) *verb* — **to drive away; scatter**
  Other form: Dispelled *(adj)*
  Sentence: The meeting served to *dispel* any fears that we were about to be fired.

DISREPUTE (diss-reh-PYOOT) *noun* — **having a poor reputation; dishonor**
  Other forms: Disreputable *(adj);* disreputability *(noun)*
  Sentence: Once a respected business, it has fallen into *disrepute*.

DISSEMBLE (dih-SEM-bull) *verb* — **to behave in a dishonest or deceitful manner**
  Other forms: Dissembling *(adj);* dissemblingly *(adv)*
  Sentence: She grew tired of her husband's *dissembling* and cheating.

DISSEMINATE (dih-SEM-ih-nate) *verb* — **to distribute widely; spread out**
  Other form: Dissemination *(noun)*
  Sentence: We can email everyone at once and *disseminate* the news quickly.

DISSIPATE (DISS-ih-pate) *verb* — **to expand and thin out indefinitely; scatter**
  Other forms: Dissipation *(noun);* dissipative *(adj)*
  Sentence: Once the sun came out, the fog *dissipated* and we could see again.

DISSONANCE (DISS-uh-nents) *noun* — **absence of harmony; discord; disagreement**
  Other forms: Dissonant *(adj);* dissonantly *(adv)*
  Sentence: Members of the audience stood to speak, and the *dissonance* was obvious.

DISSUADE (dih-SWADE) *verb* — **to advise against; discourage; deter**
  Other forms: Dissuasive *(adj);* dissuasively *(adv);* dissuasion *(noun)*
  Sentence: We tried to *dissuade* him from going, but he wouldn't listen.

DISTRAUGHT (diss-TRAWT) *adj* — **deeply troubled; frantic**
  Other form: Distraughtly *(adv)*
  Sentence: The little girl was *distraught* when she learned the dog had died.

DIURNAL (dye-URN-al) *adj* — **occurring during the day; part of a daily cycle**
Other form: Diurnally *(adv)*
Sentence: Most flowers are *diurnal*, opening with the sun and closing up at dark.

DIVEST (dy-VEST) *verb* — **to strip, especially of possessions; discard**
Other form: Divestiture *(noun)*
Sentence: In order to qualify for the program, he had to *divest* himself of all assets.

DIVISIVE (dih-VY-siv) *adj* — **tending to split; causing disunity**
Other forms: Divisively *(adv)*; divisiveness *(noun)*
Sentence: Her remarks were *divisive*, and did nothing to settle the argument.

DIVULGE (dih-VULJ) *verb* — **to make known; reveal**
Other form: Divulgence *(noun)*
Sentence: I asked him not to *divulge* my secret, and he agreed to keep quiet.

DOCILE (DAH-sill) *adj* — **obedient; passive; submissive**
Other forms: Docilely *(adv)*; docility *(noun)*
Sentence: The horse was supposed to be uncontrollable, but he was quite *docile*.

DOGGEREL (DOG-er-ul) *noun* — **unimpressive writing, especially poetry or lyrics**
Other form: Doggerel *(adj)*
Sentence: She is an excellent writer, so we were surprised by the *doggerel* she turned in.

DOLT (DOLT) *noun* — **a stupid person**
Other forms: Doltish *(adj)*; doltishly *(adv)*; doltishness *(noun)*
Sentence: Every sitcom on TV, it seems, has at least one *dolt* as a main character.

DOMICILE (DOM-ih-sile) *noun* — **a person's address, especially for legal purposes**
Other form: Domiciliary *(adj)*
Sentence: The husband and wife indicated separate *domiciles* on their tax returns.

DORMANT (DOR-ment) *adj* — **at rest; asleep; inactive**
Other form: Dormancy *(noun)*
Sentence: Microbes can remain *dormant* for years, reactivating when conditions are right.

DRAWL (DRAWL) *noun* — **slow way of speaking in which vowels are drawn out**
Other forms: Drawl (*verb*); drawling (*adj*); drawlingly (*adv*)
Sentence: His Texas *drawl* was obvious the minute he began to speak.

DRONE (DRONE) *noun* — **to speak at great length in a dull monotone**
Other form: Dronc (*verb*)
Sentence: The speaker *droned* on for several hours, while most of the audience slept.

DUBIOUS (DOO-bee-uss) *adj* — **unlikely; unsure; doubtful**
Other forms: Dubiously (*adv*); dubiousness (*noun*)
Sentence: Their story sounded far-fetched, and we were *dubious* about it.

DULCET (DUL-set) *adj* — **sweet and pleasing, especially to the ears**

Sentence: The prospect of hearing her *dulcet* voice sustained me through the ordeal.

DUPLICITY (doo-PLISS-ih-tee) *noun* — **pretense; deceit; a two-faced manner**
Other forms: Duplicitous (adj); Duplicitously *(adv)*
Sentence: A master of *duplicity*, he fooled us into thinking he was sincere.

DURESS (der-ESS) *noun* — **pressure in the form of a threat; hardship; force**
Sentence: His confession was given under *duress*: the police had threatened him.

DUTIFUL (DOOT-ih-ful) *adj* — **doing what is expected; obedient**
Other forms: Dutifulness (*noun*); dutifully (*adv*)
Sentence: He was tired of being the *dutiful* son, always doing the right thing.

DYNAMIC (dy-NAM-ik) *adj* — **highly active; full of energy; lively**
Other form: Dynamically *(adv)*
Sentence: The play was *dynamic* to watch, but was also full of insight.

EBULLIENT (eh-BULL-yent) *adj* — **enthusiastic; exuberant**
Other forms: Ebullience (*noun*); ebulliently *(adv)*
Sentence: After winning the award, the actor was *ebullient* in his acceptance speech.

ECSTATIC (ek-STAT-ik) *adj* — **without the ability to think rationally as a result of extreme physical sensation, usually pleasure or joy; rapturous**
Other form: Ecstasy (*noun*)
Sentence: We were *ecstatic* about winning the cruise, and forgot it was hurricane season.

EDACIOUS (ee-DAY-shuss) *adj* — **related to eating, especially in a voracious manner**
Other form: Edacity (*noun*)
Sentence: The termites launched an *edacious* attack on the structure of the house.

EDIBLE (EDD-ih-bull) *adj* — **suitable for eating**
Other form: Edibility *(noun)*
Sentence: Some mushrooms are *edible*, but this one is poisonous.

EDICT (EE-dikt) *noun* — **a command given by high authority**
Other forms: Edictal *(adj)*; edictally *(adv)*
Sentence: The school board issued an *edict* that no one graduates without passing the test.

EDUCE (ee-DOOS) *verb* — **to draw out; extract**
Other forms: Educible (*adj*); eduction (*noun*)
Sentence: The film's musical score *educes* a range of emotions from the viewer.

EFFETE (uh-FEET) *adj* — **drained of energy, character, or drive**
Other forms: Effetely *(adv)*; effeteness (*noun*)
Sentence: Every generation thinks the next one is lazy, *effete*, and undisciplined.

EFFICACIOUS (eff-ih-KAY-shuss) *adj* — **able to create a desired result**
Other forms: Efficaciously (adv); efficacy (*noun*)
Sentence: The new machines will be *efficacious* in improving productivity.

EFFLUVIA (eh-FLOO-vee-uh) *plural noun* — **by-product, usually as waste; exhaust**
Other form: Effluvium (*singular noun*)
Sentence: Each day, the ferry's *effluvia* include an oil slick and a ton of trash.

EFFRONTERY (uh-FRUNT-er-ee) *noun* — **rudely aggressive**
Sentence: His boldness and *effrontery* offended everyone.

EGREGIOUS (uh-GREE-juss) *adj* — **conspicuous in a negative way; flagrant**
Other forms: Egregiously *(adv);* egregiousness *(noun)*
Sentence: It was an *egregious* mistake, and we never recovered from it.

EGRESS (EE-gress) *noun* — **a means of leaving; exit**
Other form: Egression *(noun);* egressive *(adj);*
Sentence: As soon as I board a plane, I look for the nearest place of *egress*.

ELABORATE (uh-LAB-er-ayt) *verb* — **to discuss in detail; explain**
Other forms: Elaborate *(adj)* – complex or detailed; elaboration *(noun)*
Sentence: I don't understand what you mean. Could you *elaborate* a little?

ELEGY (EL-uh-jee) *noun* — **a poem or song that expresses sorrow**
Other forms: Elegiac *(adj);* elegize *(verb)*
Sentence: The song was written as an *elegy* in her honor.

ELICIT (ee-LISS-it) *verb* — **to draw forth; to bring out**
Other form: Elicitation *(noun)*
Sentence: She did her best to *elicit* a response, but I refused to talk.

ELUCIDATE (ee-LOOS-uh-dayt) *verb* — **to make clear through explanation**
Other forms: Elucidation *(noun);* elucidative *(adj)*
Sentence: Your explanation helped to *elucidate* the theory, and now I understand.

ELUDE (ee-LOOD) *verb* — **to escape capture**
Other forms: Elusive *(adj);* elusiveness *(noun)*
Sentence: The fugitive managed to *elude* the police for weeks.

EMACIATED (uh-MACE-ee-ay-tid) *adj* — **wasted away; shriveled**
Other forms: Emaciate *(verb);* emaciation *(noun)*
Sentence: Before they died, the starving dinosaurs must have looked *emaciated*.

EMANCIPATE (uh-MAN-sih-payt) *verb* — **to set free**
Other forms: Emancipation *(noun);* emancipatory *(adj)*
Sentence: Those released from slavery were *emancipated* in body, but not always in spirit.

EMBEZZLE (em-BEZZ-uhl) *verb* — **to take illegally for one's personal use**
Other form: Embezzlement *(noun)*
Sentence: The attorney *embezzled* money from his clients' estates.

EMBROIL (em-BROYL) *verb* — **to involve, especially in turmoil**
Sentence: We were tired of getting *embroiled* in his problems.

EMERITUS (e-MER-ih-tuss) *adj* — **retired after a distinguished career and now holding an honorary title**
Other form: Emeritus *(noun)*
Sentence: After retiring from the court, he became a law professor *emeritus*.

EMINENT (EM-uh-nent) *adj* — **holding a superior position; lofty**
Other forms: Eminence *(noun);* eminently *(adv)*
Sentence: Among the sumos, he held the *eminent* position and was treated with respect.

EMOTE (ee-MOTE) *verb* — **to openly express feelings**
Other forms: Emotion *(noun)*; emotive *(adj);* emotively *(adv)*
Sentence: An actor must be able to *emote* on cue.

EMPATHY (EM-puh-thee) *noun* — **the ability to experience another person's feelings**
Other form: Empathetic *(adj)*; empathize *(verb)*
Sentence: The jury must have felt *empathy*, because he was clearly guilty.

EMPIRICAL (em-PEER-uh-kul) *adj* — **relating to knowledge gained through the senses**
Other forms: Empirically *(adv);* empiricism *(noun)*
Sentence: Scientific studies must rely on *empirical* data, not wishful thinking.

ENAMOR (e-NAM-er) *verb* — **to inspire love or infatuation; to charm**
Sentence: They were *enamored* by the little village, and decided to live there.

ENCOMIUM (en-KO-mee-um) *noun* — **a formal expression of praise**
Sentence: The president's *encomium* of the ambassador was met with polite applause.

ENCORE (ON-kore) *noun* — **repeat performance, at the request of the audience**
Other form: Encore *(verb)*
Sentence: The crowd enthusiastically demanded an *encore* from the opera star.

ENCUMBER (en-KUM-ber) *verb* — **to weigh down, impede, or hamper**
Other forms: Encumbrance *(noun)*
Sentence: It's hard to swim if you're *encumbered* by clothing and shoes.

ENDEARING (en-DEER-ing) *adj* — **evoking affection or love**
Other forms: Endear *(verb)*; endearingly *(adv)*; endearment *(noun)*
Sentence: The kitten had such an *endearing* face, no one could walk away.

ENDURANCE (en-DUR-ents) *noun* — **ability to withstand hardship, stamina**
Other forms: Endure *(verb)*; enduring *(adj)*; enduringly *(adv)*
Sentence: We didn't have the *endurance* to run a marathon, and stopped after a mile.

ENDURING (en-DUR-ing) *adj* — **lasting a long time**
Other forms: Endurance *(noun)*; endure *(verb)*
Sentence: Some books have *enduring* qualities, and become classics.

ENFRANCHISE (en-FRAN-chyze) *verb* — **to endow with rights; include; set free**
Other forms: Enfranchised *(adj)*; enfranchisement *(noun)*
Sentence: With Lincoln's proclamation, the slaves became *enfranchised*, at least in theory.

ENGENDER (en-JEN-der) *verb* — **to cause to develop; inspire**
Sentence: Rather than humiliate, our boss knew how to *engender* confidence in us.

ENGRAVE (en-GRAVE) *verb* — **to impress deeply, either in a physical object or the mind**
Other forms: Engraved *(adj)*; engraver *(noun)*
Sentence: We wanted to *engrave* something meaningful onto the bracelet.

ENGULF (en-GULF) *verb* — **to overpower; overwhelm; flow over and cover**
Other form: Engulfment *(noun)*
Sentence: Within seconds the old wooden building was *engulfed* in flames.

ENJOIN (en-JOYN) *verb* — **to command with great authority; also, to forbid**
Other form: Enjoinder *(noun)*
Sentence: The United Nations *enjoined* the dictator to withdraw his troops.

ENORMITY (ee-NORM-uh-tee) *noun* — **hugeness; immensity**
Other forms: Enormous *(adj)*; enormously *(adv)*
Sentence: The *enormity* of the project would be overwhelming for most people.

ENTAIL (en-TALE) *verb* — **to require or involve**
Other form: Entailment *(noun)*
Sentence: What will this project *entail*, and when is the deadline?

ENTANGLE (en-TAN-gull) *verb* — **to snarl or interweave**
Other forms: Entangled *(adj)*; entanglement *(noun)*
Sentence: Dolphins sometimes become *entangled* in fishing nets.

ENTHRALL (en-THRAWL) *verb* — **to hold spellbound; charm; captivate**
Other forms: Enthralling *(adj)*; enthrallment *(noun)*
Sentence: As soon as the actress opened her mouth to speak, the audience was *enthralled*.

ENTOMOLOGY (en-toh-MOLL-ih-jee) *noun* — **the study of insects**
Other forms: Entomological *(adj)*; entomologist *(noun)*
Sentence: As a child, our daughter hated insects, but now she's majoring in *entomology*.

ENTREAT (en-TREET) *verb* — **humbly request; plead; beg**
Other forms: Entreatingly *(adv)*; entreaty *(noun)*
Sentence: The convicted man *entreated* the judge for mercy.

ENZYME (EN-zyme) *noun* — **protein produced in cells that triggers chemical reactions**
Other forms: Enzymatic *(adj)*; enzymatically *(adv)*
Sentence: The body produces many *enzymes* necessary for metabolism.

EPICURE (EPP-uh-kyoor) *noun* — **person with discriminating taste; connoisseur**
Other form: Epicurean *(adj)*
Sentence: She decided to record her *epicurean* gifts by writing a cookbook.

EPIGRAM (EP-ih-gram) *noun* — **a short, witty saying**
   Other forms: Epigrammatic (*adj*); epigrammatically (*adv*)
   Sentence: Many *epigrams* can be traced back to Shakespearean plays.

EPIPHANY (eh-PIFF-uh-nee) *noun* — **a sudden, clear understanding or realization**
   Sentence: Many people experience an *epiphany* at the top of a mountain.

EPISTLE (eh-PIS-uhl) *noun* — **a letter containing an important message**
   Other form: Epistolic (*adj*)
   Sentence: Long ago, an *epistle* was sent to communicate with people of far-off places.

EPITHET (EPP-ih-thet) *noun* — **word or phrase closely associated with a person or thing**
   Other form: Epithetic (*adj*)
   Sentence: Lou Gehrig earned the *epithet* Iron Man by playing even when sick or injured.

EPITOME (eh-PIT-uh-mee) *noun* — **an ideal representation of something**
   Other form: Epitomize (*verb*)
   Sentence: Albert Einstein was the *epitome* of an abstract thinker.

EQUANIMITY (eh-kwa-NIM-uh-tee) *noun* — **mental and emotional balance; composure**
   Other forms: Equanimous (*adj*); equanimously (*adv*)
   Sentence: Your *equanimity* will help you get through this crisis.

EQUILIBRIUM (ee-kwa-LIB-ree-um) *noun* — **state of balance among opposing forces**
   Other form: Equilibratory (*adj*)
   Sentence: We lose our *equilibrium* when we spin around too fast.

EQUIPOISE (EK-wah-poyz) *noun* — **balance**
   Other form: Equipoised (*adj*)
   Sentence: The two houses of parliament served as an *equipoise* for each other.

EQUITABLE (EK-wih-tah-bull) *adj* — **in a way that is fair to everyone involved**
   Other form: Equitably (*adv*)
   Sentence: The inheritance was shared in an *equitable* way among the four children.

EQUIVOCAL (ee-KWIV-uh-kul) *adj* — **having more than one interpretation; ambiguous**
    Other form: Equivocally *(adv)*
    Sentence: The decision of the court was *equivocal*, and left everyone confused.

EQUIVOCATE (ee-KWIV-uh-kayt) *verb* — **to speak in a way that is intentionally vague**
    Other form: Equivocation *(noun)*
    Sentence: A shrewd politician will *equivocate* to appeal to as many voters as possible.

ERUDITION (er-yoo-DISH-un) *noun* — **learnedness; knowledge**
    Other forms: Erudite *(adj)*; eruditely *(adv)*
    Sentence: The old scientist's *erudition* was intimidating to the younger students.

ESCHEW (es-CHOO) *verb* — **choose to avoid or abstain certain temptations; shun**
    Other form: Eschewal *(noun)*
    Sentence: The movie star *eschewed* the typical celebrity trappings, and lived simply.

ESPOUSE (es-POWZ) *verb* — **to adopt and support a belief**
    Other form: Espousal *(noun)*
    Sentence: After returning from war, he *espoused* pacifist ideasl he never had before.

ESPY (eh-SPY) *verb* — **to see something not readily obvious**
    Sentence: We *espied* the unnamed comet among a sea of stars.

ETYMOLOGY (eh-tih-MOLL-ih-jee) *noun* — **the linguistic origin of a word**
    Other forms: Etymological *(adj)*; etymologically *(adv)*; etymologist *(noun)*
    Sentence: The *etymology* of many words is rooted in old Latin.

EUPHONY (YOO-fuh-nee) *noun* — **pleasant sound; harmony**
    Other forms: Euphonious *(adj)*; euphoniously *(adv)*
    Sentence: Her speech was a *euphony* of words and sounds, enjoyed by everyone.

EUPHORIA (yoo-FOR-ee-uh) *noun* — **state of extreme well-being**
    Other form: Euphoric *(adj)*
    Sentence: Drugs elicit a short-lived feeling of *euphoria* that becomes a lifelong addiction.

EVANESCENT (ev-uh-NESS-ent) *adj* — **tending to disappear like vapor; fleeting**
    Other forms: Evanescence *(noun)*; evanescently *(adv)*
    Sentence: Our time together seemed *evanescent*, while the time apart seemed endless.

EVINCE (ee-VINCE) *verb* — **inclined toward fighting; aggressive**
    Other forms: Bellicosely *(adv)*; bellicosity *(noun)*
    Sentence: He could *evince* a warm smile from even the most unhappy.

EVOKE (eh-VOKE) *verb* — **to call forth; cause to appear; summon**
    Other forms: Evocation *(noun)*; evocative *(adj)*; evocatively *(adv)*
    Sentence: The photograph *evoked* many memories of my childhood.

EXASPERATION (egg-ZAS-per-ay-shun) *noun* — **annoyance; irritation**
    Other forms: Exasperate *(verb)*; exasperated, exasperating *(adj)*
    Sentence: It wasn't anger, exactly, but *exasperation* that I felt.

EXCAVATE (EX-kah-vayt) *verb* — **to dig out and expose to view**
    Other forms: Excavated *(adj)*; excavation *(noun)*
    Sentence: As archeologists continued to *excavate* the site, they found more bones.

EXCULPATE (EX-kul-payt) *verb* — **to free from blame or guilt; exonerate**
    Other forms: Exculpation *(noun)*; exculpatory *(adj)*
    Sentence: I'm sure the evidence will help *exculpate* me from these charges.

EXCURSION (ex-KER-zhun) *noun* — **a trip made with the intent of returning to the starting point, but perhaps with an indefinite destination**
    Other form: Excursionary *(adj)*
    Sentence: We took an *excursion* into the countryside and discovered new places.

EXECRABLE (EX-uh-kruh-bull) *adj* — **deserving of damnation; wretched; cursed**
    Other forms: Execrably *(adv)*; execrate (verb); execration *(noun)*
    Sentence: The killer's actions were *execrable*, and he deserved his punishment.

EXEGESIS (ek-suh-JEE-sis) *noun* — **explanation or interpretation of a text**
    Other forms: Exegetic *(adj)*; exegetically *(adv)*
    Sentence: Has anyone produced an *exegesis* of this cryptic book?

EXEMPLARY (ek-ZEM-pluh-ree) *adj* — **serving as a good example; commendable**
Sentence: Your essay is *exemplary* and I want your classmates to hear it.

EXHAUSTIVE (egg-ZAWS-tiv) *adj* — **thorough; complete; covering the full range**
Other form: Exhaustively *(adv)*
Sentence: After two years of *exhaustive* research, we had found no new information.

EXHORT (egg-ZORT) *verb* — **to urge strongly**
Other forms: Exhortation *(noun);* exhortative *(adj)*
Sentence: The coach *exhorted* his team, but they were clearly overmatched.

EXHUME (egg-ZOOM) *verb* — **to dig up, especially out of the ground; disinter**
Other form: Exhumation *(noun)*
Sentence: Having the body *exhumed* would be emotionally difficult for the family.

EXIGENCY (egg-ZIH-jen-see) *noun* — **situation requiring immediate action**
Other forms: Exigent *(adj);* exigently *(adv)*
Sentence: It was clear from the damage that the city was not prepared for any *exigency*.

EXISTENTIAL (egg-ziss-TEN-chull) *adj* — **related to the realities of existence and life**
Other forms: Existentialism, existentialist *(nouns)*
Sentence: As he grew older, his philosophy drifted toward the *existential*.

EXONERATE (egg-ZAHN-er-ayt) *verb* — **to free from guilt; vindicate**
Other form: Exoneration *(noun)*
Sentence: Rather than prove their case, the prosecutors inadvertently *exonerated* him.

EXORBITANT (egg-ZOR-bih-tent) *adj* — **dramatically exceeding normal limits**
Other forms: Exorbitance *(noun);* exorbitantly *(adv)*
Sentence: Shocked by the *exorbitant* prices, I reluctantly pulled out my wallet.

EXPATIATE (ex-PAY-she-ayt) *verb* — **to elaborate; explain in detail**
Other form: Expatiation *(noun)*
Sentence: Once out of office, political leaders have more time to *expatiate* on past events.

EXPATRIATE (ex-PAY-tree-ayt) *verb* — **to leave one's country of citizenship**
Other forms: Expatriate *(adj);* expatriate *(noun);* expatriation *(noun)*
Sentence: We are British citizens who chose to *expatriate* to China.

EXPEDIENT (ex-PEED-ee-yent) *adj* — **producing the quickest means to an end**
Other forms: Expediency *(noun);* expediently *(adv);* expedite *(verb)*
Sentence: It would be more *expedient* to use email, rather than the post office.

EXPEDITE (EX-peh-dite) *verb* — **to complete promptly**
Other forms: Expediency, expedition *(nouns);* expedient *(adj);* expediently *(adv)*
Sentence: We could *expedite* this project by talking less and working more.

EXPIATE (EX-pee-yate) *verb* — **to make amends for past deeds; atone**
Other forms: Expiation *(noun);* expiative, expiatory *(adj)*
Sentence: He tried to *expiate* his guilt by volunteering in the community.

EXPOSTULATE (ex-PAHS-choo-layt) *verb* — **to explain an objection; protest**
Other forms: Expostulation *(noun);* expostulatory *(adj)*
Sentence: We tried to *expostulate* the command, but our arguments were ignored.

EXSCIND (ek-SIND) *verb* — **to cut out; delete**
Sentence: Inexplicably, paragraphs that would have clarified the text were *exscinded*.

EXTANT (EX-tant) *adj* — **still in existence**
Sentence: Many artifacts from Pompeii are *extant* because they were preserved in ash.

EXTEMPORE (ex-TEMP-or-ay) *adj* — **unplanned; improvised; impromptu**
Other forms: Extemporaneous *(adj);* extemporaneously *(adv);* extemporize *(verb)*
Sentence: The trip was *extempore*: we decided to go at the last minute.

EXTENUATE (ex-TEN-yoo-ayt) *verb* — **to offer excuses for an offense in order to make it appear less serious**
Other forms: Extenuating *(adj);* extenuation *(noun)*
Sentence: He admitted to the crime, but said there were *extenuating* circumstances.

EXTINCT (ek-STINKT) *adj* — **no longer living; died out completely as a group**
Other form: Extinction (*noun*)
Sentence: Can we use DNA to recreate an animal that is *extinct*?

EXTINGUISH (ex-TING-gwish) *verb* — **to stop from burning; smother; destroy**
Other form: Extinguishable *(adj)*
Sentence: It's important to *extinguish* all fires before leaving a campsite.

EXTIRPATE (EX-ter-payt) *verb* — **to pull out; exterminate; eradicate**
Other form: Extirpation *(noun)*
Sentence: Entire species of plants and animals have been *extirpated* by the fire.

EXTORT (ex-TORT) *verb* — **to obtain through force, threat, or trickery**
Other forms: Extortion *(adv)*; extortionary *(adj)*
Sentence: He knew a secret about his boss and tried to *extort* money from him.

EXTRUDE (ex-TROOD) *verb* — **to force through an opening; to shape by squeezing**
Other forms: Extrusion (*noun*); extrusive *(adj)*
Sentence: Glass is *extruded*, stretched, and cut to make filaments.

FABRICATE (FAB-rih-kayt) *verb* — **to manufacture; make up a story to deceive**
Other form: Fabrication *(noun)*
Sentence: The little boy had *fabricated* the story in order to avoid being punished.

FACETIOUS (fuh-SEE-shuss) *adj* — **witty; joking playfully**
Other forms: Facetiousness *(noun)*; facetiously *(adv)*
Sentence: His *facetious* comments soon became sarcastic, and then cruel.

FACILE (FASS-il) *adj* — **easily accomplished; superficial**
Other forms: Facilely (adv); facility *(noun)*
Sentence: Your report, while well-written, is *facile* and unacceptable

FACTION (FAK-shun) *noun* — **a small group in dispute with another**
Other forms: Bereave *(verb)*; bereavement *(noun)*
Sentence: Large groups of people usually break up into smaller *factions*.

FALTER (FALL-ter) *verb* — **to proceed with hesitation; stumble; stagger**
Other form: Falteringly *(adv)*
Sentence: He *faltered* just before the goal line and was tackled by the defense.

FATHOM (FAH-thum) *verb* — **to finally understand a deep mystery**
Other form: Fathomable *(adj)*
Sentence: It's impossible to *fathom* how big the universe is.

FATUOUS (FAT-choo-uss) *adj* — **foolish; silly; stupid**
Other form: Fatuously *(adv)*
Sentence: Often, the more intelligent we try to sound, the more *fatuous* we seem to be.

FAWN (FAWN) *verb* — **to flatter excessively; grovel**
Other form: Fawning *(adj)*
Sentence: Powerful people are often surrounded by *fawning* followers.

FEALTY (FEEL-tee) *noun* — **absolute faithfulness to an authority; allegiance**
Sentence: The new citizens pledged *fealty* to the constitution of their adopted land.

FECUND (FEK-und) *adj* — **productive; fertile**
Other form: Fecundity *(noun)*
Sentence: His *fecund* mind has produced hundreds of inventions.

FEINT (FAYNT) *verb* — **to pretend in order to distract**
Other forms: Feign *(verb);* feint *(adj);* feint *(noun)*
Sentence: The soccer player *feinted* left, then moved right, eluding his opponent.

FELICITOUS (fuh-LISS-ih-tuss) *adj* — **charming; pleasant; happy**
Other forms: Felicitate *(verb);* felicitously *(adv);* felicity *(noun)*
Sentence: Her *felicitous* manner was a facade; she was actually a bully.

FELON (FELL-in) *noun* — **person who has been convicted of a serious crime**
Other forms: Felonious *(adj);* feloniously *(adv)*
Sentence: In some countries, a convicted *felon* loses the right to vote.

FERAL (FEER-ul) *adj* — **raised in nature; wild; not domesticated or tame**
    Sentence: Most animals are inherently *feral*, and cannot be turned into house pets.

FEROCITY (fer-OSS-ih-tee) *noun* — **savageness; fury**
    Other forms: Ferocious *(adj)*; ferociously *(adv)*
    Sentence: That boxer fights with such *ferocity*, his opponents don't have a chance.

FERVID (FER-vid) *adj* — **with great heat or intensity; passionate**
    Other forms: Fervidly *(adv)*; fervor *(noun)*
    Sentence: She approached every task with a *fervid* desire to succeed.

FETID (FETT-id) *adj* — **having a bad smell**
    Other forms: Fetidly *(adv)*; fetidness *(noun)*
    Sentence: The windows hadn't been opened in months, and the air inside was *fetid*.

FETTER (FETT-er) *verb* — **to restrain; to put into shackles**
    Other forms: Fetter *(noun)*; fettered *(adj)*
    Sentence: The colonists felt *fettered* by too many laws, and grew rebellious.

FIASCO (fee-ASK-oh) *noun* — **the disastrous result of a plan or project**
    Sentence: What seemed like a good idea turned into such a *fiasco* that we abandoned it.

FIDELITY (fih-DELL-ih-tee) *noun* — **loyalty; allegiance; faithfulness**
    Sentence: The director's *fidelity* to the original story helped make the film a success.

FIDGET (FIJ-it) *verb* — **to squirm or worry incessantly; to move nervously**
    Other forms: Fidget *(noun)*; fidgety *(adj)*
    Sentence: The speaker was so nervous, he couldn't stop *fidgeting* and pacing.

FIGURATIVE (FIG-yer-uh-tiv) *adj* — **made abstract through symbol, metaphor, etc.**
    Other form: Figuratively *(adv)*; figurativeness *(noun)*
    Sentence: My example was *figurative*; I didn't mean it literally.

FINESSE (fih-NESS) *noun* — **artful maneuvering; refined skill**
Other form: Finesse *(verb)*
Sentence: She plays the game with such *finesse*, as if she could do it with her eyes closed.

FISSION (FISH-un) *noun* — **the process of breaking apart or splitting**
Other form: Fission *(verb)*
Sentence: Huge amounts of energy are released during *fission*, when atoms are split.

FITFUL (FIT-ful) *adj* — **variable; spasmodic; unstable**
Other forms: Fitfully *(adv)*; fitfulness *(noun)*
Sentence: I slept *fitfully* because of the noises out in the street.

FLABBERGASTED (FLAB-er-gass-ted) *adj* — **overwhelmed with surprise**
Other form: Flabbergast *(verb)*
Sentence: We were *flabbergasted* to see giraffes parading down the street.

FLAMBOYANT (flam-BOY-ent) *adj* — **wildly showy; ostentatious**
Other forms: Flamboyance *(noun)*; flamboyantly *(adv)*
Sentence: His *flamboyant* costumes and wild hair are part of his act.

FLAUNT (FLAWNT) *verb* — **to parade oneself around to attract attention**
Other form: Flauntingly *(adv)*
Sentence: They like to *flaunt* their wealth and make their neighbors envious.

FLAX (FLAKS) *noun* — **a plant used in the manufacture of linen**
Sentence: *Flax* goes through several steps before it can be turned into fabric.

FLINCH (FLINCH) *verb* — **to pull back by reflex; to tense and withdraw; recoil**
Other form: Flinchingly *(adv)*
Sentence: The pitch sailed very close to the batter's head, but he never *flinched*.

FLORID (FLOR-id) *adj* — **flushed; tinged with red; ruddy**
Other forms: Floridity *(noun)*; floridly *(adv)*
Sentence: Our faces were *florid* from the cold air.

FLOUT (FLOWT) *verb* — **to mock or insult; scoff**
    Other form: Floutingly *(adv)*
    Sentence: He openly *flouted* the law, but never seemed to get into trouble.

FLUSTER (FLUSS-ter) *verb* — **to put into a state of confusion; muddle**
    Other forms: Fluster *(noun);* flustrated *(adj)*
    Sentence: She tried to *fluster* me with her questions, but I couldn't be rattled.

FLUX (FLUKS) *noun* — **in a flowing or changing state**
    Other forms: Flux, fluxible *(adj)*; flux *(verb)*
    Sentence: Politically, the nation was in *flux* and nobody knew how it would turn out.

FOIBLE (FOY-bull) *noun* — **a minor flaw, usually in a person's character; fault**
    Sentence: A husband and wife must learn to live with each other's *foibles*.

FOIL (FOYL) *verb* — **to spoil a plan; to prevent**
    Other forms: Foil *(noun);* foiled *(adj)*
    Sentence: The police managed to *foil* the bank robber's plan by setting a trap.

FOPPISH (FOPP-ish) *adj* — **a man who is overly vain about his appearance**
    Other form: Fop *(noun)*
    Sentence: His character was *foppish*, but in real life the actor was plain and modest.

FORAGE (FOR-ej) *verb* — **to wander and search for, especially food or supplies**
    Other form: Forage *(noun)*
    Sentence: Squirrels must *forage* for food before the winter sets in.

FORBEARANCE (for-BARE-ents) *noun* — **tolerance; leniency; patience**
    Other forms: Forbear *(verb)*; forbearing *(adj);* forbearingly *(adv)*
    Sentence: We had no money for rent, helped only by our landlord's *forbearance*.

FORD (FORD) *verb* — **to cross a river or stream, usually by wading**
    Other form: Fordable *(adj)*
    Sentence: Sometimes *fording* a river at a wide point is easier because the water is calmer.

FORESTALL (for-STAWL) *verb* — **to prevent or take advantage of by anticipation**
Other form: Forestalling *(adj)*; forestallment *(noun)*
Sentence: He *forestalled* complete financial ruin by selling his shares early.

FORFEIT (FOR-fit) *verb* — **to give up or lose because of some offense or neglect**
Other form: Forfeit, forfeiture *(nouns)*
Sentence: The soccer team had to *forfeit* the game because it didn't have enough players.

FORGERY (FOR-juh-ree) *noun* — **a false representation, such as a fake signature**
Other forms: Forge *(verb)*; forger *(noun)*
Sentence: The handwriting expert declared the signature to be a *forgery*.

FORLORN (for-LORN) *adj* — **abandoned and miserable; lonely; despondent**
Other form: Forlornly *(adv)*
Sentence: The dog looked so lost and *forlorn* that we just had to take him home.

FORMIDABLE (FOR-mid-uh-bull) *adj* — **inspiring awe; intimidating; superior**
Other forms: Formidableness *(noun)*; formidably *(adv)*
Sentence: It must have been a *formidable* task to build a castle on top of a mountain.

FORSWEAR (for-SWARE) *verb* — **to openly and loudly reject, sometimes under oath**
Sentence: He *forswore* to ever smoke again, and we believed him.

FORTIFY (FORT-ih-fye) *verb* — **to add strength; to build up in structure or content**
Other forms: Fortification *(noun)*; fortified *(adj)*
Sentence: Many processed foods are *fortified* with extra vitamins.

FORTITUDE (FORT-ih-tood) *noun* — **strength of character needed to endure hardship**
Other form: Fortitudinous *(adj)*
Sentence: Thay went through a lot of pain, but had the *fortitude* to go on.

FORTUITOUS (for-TOO-ih-tuss) *adj* — **through luck or chance**
Other forms: Fortuitously *(adv)*; fortuitousness *(noun)*
Sentence: It was *fortuitous* that you sent your resume the day my assistant quit.

FOSTER (FAWS-ter) *verb* — **to promote development; cultivate**
Sentence: Her generous donation has helped *foster* the project.

FRACTIOUS (FRAK-chuss) *adj* — **uncontrollable; rebellious; unruly**
Other forms: Fractiously (*adv*); fractiousness (*noun*)
Sentence: Most of the kids were well-behaved, but one was *fractious* and quarrelsome.

FRAGILE (FRAH-jil) *adj* — **easily broken; brittle, frail**
Other form: Fragility *(noun)*
Sentence: His *fragile* health was aggravated by the cold climate.

FRANTIC (FRAN-tik) *adj* — **driven by anxiety or time pressure; frenzied**
Other form: Frantically *(adv)*
Sentence: The parents became *frantic* when they couldn't find their little girl.

FRAUDULENT (FRAW-joo-lent) *adj* — **deceitful; counterfeit; misrepresentative**
Other forms: Fraud, fraudulence *(nouns);* fraudulently *(adv)*
Sentence: We were shocked to learn that all of his diplomas were *fraudulent.*

FRENETIC (fruh-NET-ik) *adj* — **in a fast and frenzied manner; chaotic**
Other form: Frenetically *(adv)*
Sentence: The activity in the office was so *frenetic*, it gave me a headache.

FRIVOLITY (frih-VOLL-ih-tee) *noun* — **silliness; insignificance; lack of seriousness**
Other forms: Frivolous *(adj);* frivolously *(adv)*
Sentence: After months of hard work, we finally had a few carefree days of *frivolity.*

FRIVOLOUS (FRIV-uh-luss) *adj* — **playful; unimportant; light-minded**
Other forms: Frivolity *(noun);* frivolously *(adv)*
Sentence: We were allowed to be *frivolous* because it was the last day of school.

FROWZY (FROW-zee) *adj* — **shabby; unkempt; disheveled**
Other form: Frowzled *(adj)*
Sentence: His *frowzy* appearance indicated that he'd been sleeping in his car.

FULSOME (FULL-sum) *adj* — **displaying extremely bad taste; repulsive**
    Other forms: Fulsomely *(adv)*; fulsomeness *(noun)*
    Sentence: His *fulsome* behavior at the wedding shocked everyone.

GAINSAY (GAIN-say) *verb* — **deny; contradict; resist**
    Sentence: To argue against this freedom is to *gainsay* everything we stand for.

GAMBOL (GAM-bull) *verb* — **to prance around happily; frolic**
    Other form: Gambol *(noun)*
    Sentence: They were *gamboling* around in the grass, seemingly without a care.

GARISH (GARE-ish) *adj* — **excessively showy or gaudy; ostentatious**
    Other forms: Garishly *(adv)*; garishness *(noun)*
    Sentence: Her *garish* style didn't fit in with the modest and conservative community.

GENTEEL (jen-TEEL) *adj* — **stylish; fashionable; aristocratic**
    Other form: Genteelness *(noun)*
    Sentence: His *genteel* clothing and manner told us he had grown up in affluence.

GESTICULATE (jes-TIK-yoo-layt) *verb* — **to motion with the body while speaking**
    Other forms: Gesticulation *(noun)*; gesticulative, gesticulatory *(adj)*
    Sentence: My grandmother could communicate with facial expressions and *gesticulation*.

GIST (JIST) *noun* — **the main point or idea; essence**
    Sentence: I listened to the physicist's speech, but got only the *gist* of it.

GLACIAL (GLAY-shul) *adj* — **with extreme slowness**
    Other form: Glacially *(adv)*
    Sentence: The approval process moves at a *glacial* pace, and we could not wait.

GLIMMER (GLIM-er) *noun* — **a faint glow; a trace**
    Other forms: Glimmering, glimmery *(adv)*
    Sentence: We were all discouraged, but he had a *glimmer* of hope in his eyes.

GLOAT (GLOTE) *verb* — **to excessively celebrate a victory; exult; revel**
Other forms: Gloat *(noun)*; gloatingly *(adv)*
Sentence: It's a sign of poor sportsmanship to *gloat* after winning a game.

GLUT (GLUT) *noun* — **abundance; oversupply**
Other forms: Glut *(verb)*; glutton, gluttony *(nouns)*
Sentence: A *glut* of corn on the market caused the prices to drop.

GOAD (GODE) *verb* — **prod; motivate; urge**
Other form: Goad *(noun)*
Sentence: Sometimes the *goading* of a group can get you to do something unexpected.

GOSSAMER (GAHS-uh-mer) *adj* — **delicate; flimsy; tenuous**
Other form: Gossamer *(noun)*
Sentence: His *gossamer* alibi would never stand up to scrutiny.

GOURMAND (GOR-mand) *noun* — **one who is fond of eating; connoisseur**
Other form: Gourmand *(adj)*
Sentence: We were nervous about dinner: one of the guests was a real *gourmand*.

GRANDILOQUENT (gran-DILL-uh-kwent) *adj* — **magnificently boastful; pompous**
Other forms: Grandiloquence *(noun);* grandiloquently *(adv)*
Sentence: She was so caught up in her own *grandiloquence*, she hardly noticed us.

GRANDIOSE (GRAN-dee-ose) *adj* — **large and exaggerated in order to impress**
Other forms: Grandiosely *(adv);* grandiosity *(noun)*
Sentence: The statue was *grandiose*, and seemed wrong for such a confined space.

GRATUITOUS (gruh-TOO-ih-tuss) *adj* — **unnecessary; unwarranted**
Other forms: Gratuitously *(adv);* gratuitousness *(noun)*
Sentence: His *gratuitous* remarks about women bothered many in the audience.

GRIEVOUS (GREE-vuss) *adj* — **causing great suffering; burdensome**
Other forms: Grievously *(adv);* grievousness *(noun)*
Sentence: Conditions after the earthquake were made more *grievous* by the flooding.

GROTESQUE (gro-TESK) *adj* — **unnatural; bizarre**
    Other forms: Grotesquely (*adv*); grotesqueness (*noun*)
    Sentence: The bank robbers wore *grotesque* masks so they wouldn't be recognized.

GROTTO (GROTT-oh) *noun* — **a covered or arched opening in the earth; cave**
    Sentence: We climbed through a hole and entered a beautiful *grotto* filled with water.

GUILE (GYL) *noun* — **craft and trickery; deceit**
    Other forms: Guileful (*adj*); guilefully *(adv);*
    Sentence: He was charming and full of *guile*, and we didn't trust him for a minute.

GUILELESS (GYL-less) *adj* — **naïve; innocent; unsophisticated**
    Other forms: Guilelessly *(adv);* guilelessness (*noun*)
    Sentence: Her *guileless* manner made her a prime target for scammers.

HAGGARD (HAGG-erd) *adj* — **worn out; emaciated; exhausted**
    Other forms: Haggardly (*adv*); haggardness (*noun*)
    Sentence: He'd been in the woods for weeks, and was found *haggard* and near death.

HALCYON (HAL-see-in) *adj* — **peaceful; serene**
    Sentence: Busy at school, I missed the *halcyon* days of summer.

HALLOW (HAL-oh) *verb* — **to make holy or sacred; consecrate**
    Other forms: Hallowed *(adj);* hallowedness (*noun*)
    Sentence: Most cultures treat burial places as *hallowed* ground.

HAPLESS (HAP-less) *adj* — **having chronic bad luck**
    Other forms: Haplessly (*adv*); haplessness (*noun*)
    Sentence: The *hapless* man got three flat tires in one week.

HARBINGER (HAR-bin-jer) *noun* — **something that foreshadows the future; omen**
    Other form: Harbinger *(verb)*
    Sentence: To superstitious people, almost anything can been as a *harbinger* of something.

HARROW (HAH-roh) *verb* — **to cause great suffering; to create agony**
 Other form: Harrowing *(adj)*
 Sentence: The young children were *harrowed* by the older boys' ghost stories.

HAUGHTY (HAW-tee) *adj* — **obnoxiously proud; arrogrant**
 Other form: Haughtily *(adv);* haughtiness *(noun)*
 Sentence: Her *haughty* manner made others feel inferior at first, then resentful.

HEDONISM (HEED-un-iz-um) *noun* — **pursuit of pleasure or happiness as a way of life**
 Other forms: Hedonist *(noun);* hedonistic *(adj)*
 Sentence: Many cult members end up feeding the leader's *hedonism*.

HENCHMAN (HENCH-man) *noun* — **an evil person's assistant or right-hand man**
 Sentence: The gangster gave the orders and his *henchmen* carried them out.

HERMETIC (her-MET-ik) *adj* — **airtight; impervious to outside influence**
 Other form: Hermetically *(adv)*
 Sentence: Fearing a riot, the police created an *hermetic* field around the prison.

HETEROGENEOUS (het-er-oh-JEEN-ee-us) *adj* — **made up of differing parts; disparate**
 Other forms: Heterogeneously *(adv);* heterogeneousness *(noun)*
 Sentence: Most big cities have *heterogeneous* populations, with many immigrants.

HIRSUTE (her-SOOT) *adj* — **hairy; shaggy; having to do with hair**
 Other form: Hirsuteness *(noun)*
 Sentence: Some dogs are very *hirsute*, while others have no hair at all.

HISTRIONIC (hiss-tree-ON-ik) *adj* — **exaggeratedly theatrical; melodramatic**
 Other forms: Histrionically *(adv);* histrionics *(noun)*
 Sentence: Her *histrionics* after such a minor accident were hard to fathom.

HOODWINK (HOOD-wink) *verb* — **to fool; to dupe**
 Other form: Hoodwink *(noun)*
 Sentence: We felt *hoodwinked* by the advertiser's false claims.

HOSPITABLE (ha-SPIT-uh-bull) *adj* — **welcoming; friendly to guests; cordial**
Other form: Hospitably *(adv)*
Sentence: They had a reputation for being cold, but were most *hospitable* to us.

HUBRIS (HYU-briss) *noun* — **excessive self-confidence; arrogance**
Other form: Hubristic *(adj)*; hubristically *(adv)*
Sentence: Our family tends to be modest, so my cousin's *hubris* was unexpected.

HYPOTHESIS (hy-puh-THET-ih-kul) *noun* — **idea to be tested; assumption**
Other forms: Hypothesize *(verb);* hypothetical *(adj)*; hypothetically *(adv)*
Sentence: Upon investigation, the girl's *hypothesis* proved correct.

ICONOCLAST (eye-KAHN-uh-klast) *noun* — **one who attacks or rejects accepted beliefs, customs, or institutions**
Other form: Iconoclastic *(adj)*
Sentence: He wasn't really an *iconoclast*, but he liked the attention given to rebels.

IDIOSYNCRASY (id-ee-oh-SIN-kruh-see) *noun* — **something peculiar to an individual**
Other form: Idiosyncratic *(adj)*
Sentence: After a while, someone's *idiosyncrasies* can become endearing, or annoying.

IDIOSYNCRATIC (id-ee-oh-sin-KRAT-ik) *adj* — **eccentric; characteristic**
Other form: Idiosyncrasy *(noun)*
Sentence: The howling you hear is *idiosyncratic* of a certain type of monkey.

IDYLLIC (eye-DILL-ik) *adj* — **a state of dreamy pleasantness; paradise-like**
Other form: Idyll *(noun)*
Sentence: It was shocking to hear of a murder taking place in such an *idyllic* setting.

IGNOBLE (igg-NO-bel) *adj* — **base; unworthy of praise**
Other form: Ignobility *(noun)*
Sentence: His motives were *ignoble* at best, and perhaps even criminal.

IGNOMINIOUS (igg-no-MIN-ee-us) *adj* — **deserving of shame; disgraceful**
Other forms: Ignominiously *(adv);* ignominy *(noun)*
Sentence: The deposed dictator lived his last years in exile, and *ignominious* poverty.

ILLICIT (ill-LISS-it) *adj* — **not permitted; illegal**
    Other form: Illicitly *(adv)*
    Sentence: He was caught selling *illicit* drugs and is now serving time in prison.

ILLUSORY (ih-LOOZ-uh-ree) *adj* — **falsely appearing real; deceptive**
    Other forms: Illusion *(noun)*; illusorily *(adv)*
    Sentence: Their reconciliation was *illusory*: they resumed fighting almost immediately.

IMBROGLIO (im-BROLE-yo) *noun* — **wild and violent confrontation**
    Sentence: The *imbroglio* in the bar had started as an innocent disagreement.

IMBRUE (im-BREW) *verb* — **to soak**
    Sentence: Her pillow was *imbrued* with her tears.

IMMACULATE (ih-MAK-yoo-let) *adj* — **pure; unspoiled; spotless**
    Other forms: Immaculately *(adv);* immaculateness *(noun)*
    Sentence: The dress came back from the dry cleaner in *immaculate* condition.

IMMERSE (ih-MERSE) *verb* — **to plunge into deeply, as in a liquid or a subject**
    Other forms: Immersible *(adj)*; immersion *(noun)*
    Sentence: He had been so *immersed* in his book that he never heard me come in.

IMPECCABLE (im-PEK-uh-bull) *adj* — **perfect; flawless**
    Other forms: Impeccability *(noun);* impeccably *(adv)*
    Sentence: Just two years after arriving, her mastery of the language was *impeccable*.

IMPECUNIOUS (im-peh-KYOO-nee-us) *adj* — **penniless; indigent**
    Other forms: Impecuniously *(adv);* impecuniousness *(noun)*
    Sentence: He made millions in business, but ended up *impecunious* and homeless.

IMPERATIVE (im-PER-ih-tiv) *adj* — **forceful; commanding, required**
    Other forms: Imperative *(noun);* imperatively *(adv)*
    Sentence: We thought our attendance was voluntary, but the teacher said it was *imperative*.

IMPERIOUS (im-PEER-ee-us) *adj* — **domineering; overbearing**
Other forms: Imperiously *(adv);* imperiousness *(noun)*
Sentence: The classroom was his domain and he ruled it with an *imperious* tone.

IMPERTURBABLE (im-per-TER-buh-bull) *adj* — **unflappable; immune to bother**
Other forms: Imperturbability *(noun);* imperturbably *(adv)*
Sentence: She claimed to be *imperturbable*, but we managed to upset her once or twice.

IMPERVIOUS (im-PER-vee-us) *adj* — **not capable of being affected or penetrated**
Other forms: Imperviously *(adv);* imperviousness *(noun)*
Sentence: With walls ten feet thick, the fortress was *impervious* to attack.

IMPIETY (im-PYE-ih-tee) *noun* — **lack of respect or obedience, usually toward a religious doctrine**
Other forms: Impious *(adj);* impiously *(adv)*
Sentence: For a minister, his speech showed a level of *impiety* that surprised us.

IMPLACABLE (im-PLAK-uh-bull) *adj* — **not able to be appeased or relieved**
Other forms: Implacability *(noun);* implacably *(adv)*
Sentence: We were unable to ease her *implacable* grief.

IMPLICATE (IM-plih-kayt) *verb* — **to involve, usually in an unfavorable way**
Other form: Implication *(noun)*
Sentence: As it turned out, the entire staff was *implicated* in the cover-up.

IMPLICIT (im-PLISS-it) *adj* — **understood to be true, though not openly expressed**
Other forms: Implicitly *(adv);* implicitness *(noun)*
Sentence: His threat was *implicit*, although he never uttered the words.

IMPORTUNE (im-por-TOON) *verb* — **to plead repeatedly and aggressively; to pressure**
Other forms: Importunate *(adj);* importunately *(adv);* importunity *(noun)*
Sentence: They *importuned* us to visit, but we could never find the time.

IMPRECATION (im-preh-KAY-shun) *noun* — **curse; malediction**
Other forms: Imprecate *(verb);* imprecatingly *(adv)*
Sentence: The prisoner screamed *imprecations* at the police as they arrested him.

IMPREGNABLE (im-PREG-nuh-bull) *adj* — **incapable of being overtaken; unassailable**
Other forms: Impregnability (*noun*); impregnably (*adv*)
Sentence: The fortress was *impregnable*, and never fell into enemy hands.

IMPROMPTU (im-PROM-tu) *adj* — **on the spur of the moment; without planning**
Other forms: Impromptu *(adv);* impromptu *(noun);* impromptu *(verb)*
Sentence: The three musicians got up on stage for an *impromptu* performance.

IMPUGN (im-PYOON) *verb* — **to call into question; to deny**
Other forms: Impugnable (*adj*); impugnation (*noun*)
Sentence: I resent that you are trying to *impugn* my good reputation with idle gossip.

IMPUTE (im-PYOOT) *verb* — **to attribute, ascribe, or insinuate**
Other forms: Imputable *(adj);* imputation *(noun)*
Sentence: My aunt always *imputed* good manners to me, and eventually she was right.

INARTICULATE (in-ar-TIK-yoo-lit) *adj* — **incapable of speaking clearly; incoherent**
Other forms: Inarticulately *(adv);* inarticulateness *(noun)*
Sentence: We were so excited we became *inarticulate*, and had to communicate with notes.

INCANDESCENT (in-kan-DESS-ent) *adj* — **brightly glowing; radiant**
Other form: Incandescence *(noun)*
Sentence: The actress had an *incandescent* personality that lit up the stage.

INCANTATION (in-kan-TAY-shun) *noun* — **words used to invoke a magic spell; charm**
Other form: Incant *(verb)*
Sentence: The holy man uttered some incantations and sent the sick child on his way.

INCENDIARY (in-SEN-dee-ayr-ee) *adj* — **capable of producing fire or explosion; volatile**
Other form: Incendiary *(noun)*
Sentence: An *incendiary* device was found in the building and everyone was evacuated.

INCENSE (in-SENSE) *verb* — **to arouse extreme anger**
Other form: Incensed *(adj)*
Sentence: We were *incensed* when we heard the flight would be delayed six hours.

INCIPIENT (in-SIP-ee-ent) *adj* — **in the early stage of development; initial**
    Other forms: Incipiency (*noun*); incipiently (*adv*)
    Sentence: We could tell that he was an *incipient* scientist, even at such a young age.

INCISIVE (in-SY-siv) *adj* — **sharp; keen; able to penetrate deeply**
    Other forms: Incisively *(adv);* incisiveness *(noun)*
    Sentence: Her interpretation was *incisively* clear and to the point.

INCLINATION (in-klih-NAY-shun) *noun* — **a strong tendency; propensity**
    Other forms: Inclinable, inclined *(adj)*
    Sentence: If your *inclination* is in drama, you should pursue it wholeheartedly.

INCOHERENCE (in-ko-HEER-ents) *noun* — **a lack of consistency or clarity**
    Other forms: Incoherent (*adj*); incoherently (*adv*)
    Sentence: Your writing skills are weakened by *incoherence*; the ideas are not clear.

INCONSEQUENTIAL (in-kahn-suh-KWEN-shul) *adj* — **unimportant; trivial**
    Other forms: Inconsequence (noun); inconsequentially *(adv)*
    Sentence: The judge felt the infraction was *inconsequential*, and she let us go.

INCONTROVERTIBLE (in-kahn-truh-VERT-ih-bull) *adj* — **not open to question; sure**
    Other form: Incontrovertibly *(adv)*
    Sentence: That the planets revolve around the sun is now an *incontrovertible* fact.

INCULCATE (in-KUL-kayt) *verb* — **to impart knowledge through repetition; instill**
    Other forms: Inculcation (*noun*); inculcative (*adj*)
    Sentence: Our parents *inculcated* ethics in us by daily reminders and examples.

INCURSION (in-KUR-zhun) *noun* — **hostile penetration; invasion**
    Other forms: Incursionary, incursive *(adj)*
    Sentence: The turning point came when our forces made an *incursion* into the capital.

INDEFATIGABLE (in-duh-FAT-ih-ka-bull) *adj* — **incapable of fatigue; untiring**
    Other forms: Indefatigableness (*noun);* indefatigably *(adv)*
    Sentence: Thanks to your *indefatigable* efforts, we have finally reached our goal.

INDELIBLE (in-DELL-ih-bull) *adj* — **cannot be erased or washed away**
Other form: Indelibility (*noun*); indelibly (*adv*)
Sentence: Meeting Mother Theresa made an *indelible* impression on the whole class.

INDIGENOUS (in-DIJ-ih-niss) *adj* — **occurring naturally in a certain region; native**
Other form: Indigenously *(adv)*
Sentence: The kangaroo, *indigenous* to Australia, has probably never lived elsewhere.

INDIGNANT (in-DIG-nent) *adj* — **angry over a specific event; resentful**
Other forms: Indignantly (*adv*); indignation (*noun*)
Sentence: The residents were *indignant* when they heard a prison was being built nearby.

INDISTINCT (in-diss-DINKT) *adj* — **not easily recognized or clearly defined; blurred**
Other forms: Indistinction *(noun)*; indistinctive *(adj)*; indistinctly *(adv)*
Sentence: The galaxy appeared in the telescope as an *indistinct* patch of light.

INDOMITABLE (in-DAHM-ih-tuh-bull) *adj* — **not able to be defeated or subdued**
Other forms: Indomitability (*noun*); indomitably *(adv)*
Sentence: His opponent was a giant, and looked *indomitable*.

INDULGENT (in-DULL-jent) *adj* — **overly permissive, tolerant, or patient**
Other form: Indulge *(adv)*; indulgence *(noun)*; indulgently *(adv)*
Sentence: She disapproved of smoking, but was *indulgent* toward her husband's habit.

INEFFABLE (in-EFF-uh-bull) *adj* — **impossible to express in words**
Other form: Ineffableness (*noun*); ineffably *(adv)*
Sentence: The environments yet to be discovered on other planets may be *ineffably* alien.

INEPT (ih-NEPT) *adj* — **lacking the required knowledge or skills; bungling; awkward**
Other forms: Ineptly *(adv)*; ineptitude, ineptness *(nouns)*
Sentence: We had been expecting an expert; what we got was an *inept* novice.

INEPTITUDE (ih-NEPT-ih-tood) *noun* — **lack of skill or knowledge; awkwardness**
Other forms: Inept (*adj*); ineptly *(adv)*; ineptness (*noun*)
Sentence: He claimed to be highly-experienced, but his *ineptitude* was readily apparent.

INEVITABLE (in-EV-ih-tuh-bull) *adj* — **unavoidable; certain to occur**
Other forms: Inevitability *(noun);* inevitably *(adv)*
Sentence: Astronomers think it's *inevitable* that a large object from space will hit Earth.

INEXORABLE (in-EGGS-zer-uh-bull) *adj* — **unyielding; relentless**
Other form: Inexorably *(adv)*

Sentence: They won game after game, conducting an *inexorable* pursuit of the trophy.

INFALLIBLE (in-FAL-ih-bul) *adj* — **not capable of error or misjudgment**
Other forms: Infallibility *(noun)*; infallibly *(adv)*
Sentence: A careful scrutiny of our greatest heroes reveals that no human is *infallible*.

INFUSE (in-FYOOZ) *verb* — **meddlesome; intrusive; impertinent**
Other forms: Infused *(adj)*; infusion *(noun)*
Sentence: She said she was trying to be helpful, but I found her to be *officious* and rude.

INFUSION (in-FYOO-zhun) *noun* — **the introduction or conveyance of some quality**
Other forms: Infuse *(verb)*; infused *(adj)*
Sentence: No amount of study can replace the *infusion* of knowledge we get from travel.

INGENIOUS (in-JEEN-yuss) *adj* — **extremely resourceful; inventive; brilliant**
Other forms: Ingeniously *(adv)*; ingenuity *(noun)*
Sentence: His solution was so *ingenious*, I wondered why no one else had thought of it.

INHERENT (in-HERR-int) *adj* — **part of the essence; intrinsic; native**
Other forms: Inherence *(noun)*; inherently *(adv)*
Sentence: There are advantages and disadvantages *inherent* in every method of heating.

INHIBIT (in-HIB-it) *verb* — **stifle; prevent; forbid; restrain**
Other forms: Inhibited *(adj)*; inhibition *(noun)*
Sentence: An overly-critical teacher or boss can *inhibit* a person's creativity.

INIMICAL (in-IM-ih-kull) *adj* — **in opposition; hostile; adverse**
Other form: Inimically *(adv)*
Sentence: Your rudeness is *inimical* to the friendly way we normally treat our customers.

INIMITABLE (in-IM-ih-tuh-bull) *adj* — **incapable of being copied; without peer**
Other forms: Inimitability (*noun*); inimitably *(adv)*
Sentence: She had an *inimitable* style, and we were never able to replace her.

INIQUITY (in-IK-wih-tee) *noun* — **wrongful behavior; wickedness**
Other form: Iniquitous *(adj); iniquitously (adv)*
Sentence: We knew we'd be punished for our *iniquity*, but we did it anyway.

INJUNCTION (in-JUNK-shun) *noun* — **statement that forbids something; prohibition**
Other forms: Injunct *(verb);* injunctive *(adj)*
Sentence: The court issued an *injunction* barring the press from all future sessions.

INKLING (INK-ling) *noun* — **a vague notion; a slight bit of knowledge; hint**
Sentence: She had no *inkling* of what was happening right in her own home.

INNUENDO (in-yoo-EN-doe) *noun* — **unspoken accusation; hint; gossip**
Other form: Innuendo *(verb)*
Sentence: He never came right out and accused us, but his *innuendo* was clear.

INOPPORTUNE (in-opp-er-TOON) *adj* — **at a bad time; inconvenient**
Other forms: Inopportunely *(adv);* inopportuneness *(noun)*
Sentence: We would have been happy to see them, but it was such an *inopportune* time.

INQUISITIVE (in-KWIZ-ih-tiv) *adj* — **tending to ask questions, or examine; curious**
Other forms: Inquisitively (adv); inquisitiveness (*noun*)
Sentence: She was an *inquisitive* child who grew up to be a private investigator.

INSATIABLE (in-SAY-shuh-bull) *adj* — **incapable of being satisfied; unquenchable**
Other form: Insatiability, insatiety (*nouns*); insatiably *(adv)*
Sentence: He had an *insatiable* appetite for learning and spent many hours at the library.

INSENSIBLE (in-SENS-ih-bull) *adj* — **lacking awareness or feeling**
Other forms: Insensibility *(noun);* insensibly *(adv)*
Sentence: The crocodile is an *insensible* predator, killing to survive.

INSENTIENT (in-SEN-chent) *adj* — **lacking consciousness; unthinking**
    Other form: Insentience (*noun*)
    Sentence: I couldn't get through to him; he was as *insentient* as a rock.

INSIDIOUS (in-SID-ee-uss) *adj* — **having a gradual, almost imperceptible effect**
    Other forms: Insidiously *(adv);* insidiousness *(noun)*
    Sentence: Smoking is an *insidious* killer: any one cigarette seems to cause no harm.

INSINUATE (in-SIN-yoo-ate) *verb* — **to state indirectly; suggest; hint**
    Other form: Insinuation *(noun);* insinuative *(adj)*
    Sentence: Our professor *insinuated* that we'd cheated because we both got perfect scores.

INSOUCIANT (an-SOO-see-ent) *adj* — **lacking concern; unbothered**
    Other forms: Insouciance *(noun);* insouciantly *(adv)*
    Sentence: They were such opposites: she *insouciant*, he constantly worrying.

INSTIGATE (IN-stih-gayt) *verb* — **to provoke; urge; incite**
    Other forms: Instigation *(noun);* instigative *(adj)*
    Sentence: A few men *instigated* the violence by throwing rocks and shouting obscenities.

INSULAR (INT-suh-ler) *adj* — **narrowly-focused; insulated**
    Other forms: Insularity *(noun);* insularly *(adv)*
    Sentence: Her views were *insular* and rigid, perhaps the result of living on a tiny island.

INSURGENT (in-SUR-jint) *noun* — **person who vocally opposes civil authority**
    Other forms: Insurgency *(noun);* insurgent *(adj);* insurgently *(adv)*
    Sentence: For now, the government was just keeping an eye on the *insurgents*.

INSURRECTION (in-suh-REK-shun) *noun* — **active rebellion against authority**
    Sentence: Most political leaders will react with force when dealing with an *insurrection*.

INTEGRITY (in-TEG-rih-tee) *noun* — **displaying an adherence to some code of behavior**
    Sentence: Despite temptation, she maintained her *integrity* and did the right thing.

INTEMPERANCE (in-TEM-per-et) *noun* — **lack of moderation or control; excess**
Other forms: Intemperate *(adj);* intemperately *(adv)*
Sentence: The *intemperance* of the 1920s came to a sudden end with the Depression.

INTERDICT (in-ter-DIKT) *verb* — **to prohibit or forbid, sometimes with force**
Other forms: Interdiction *(noun);* interdictory *(adj)*
Sentence: The police *interdicted* the suspect's escape by closing the bridge.

INTERIM (IN-ter-um) *noun* — **the time in between; meanwhile**
Other forms: Interim *(adj);* interim *(adv)*
Sentence: Until an election can be held, someone will have to serve in the *interim.*

INTERLOCUTOR (in-ter-LOK-yoo-ter) *noun* — **person involved in conversation**
Other forms: Interlocution *(noun);* interlocutory *(adj)*
Sentence: Intended to serve as mediator, he ended up as an *interlocutor* in the debate.

INTERMINABLE (in-TER-min-uh-bull) *adj* — **endless, or seemingly so**
Other forms: Interminableness *(noun)*; interminably *(adv)*
Sentence: When his interminable speech reached three hours, we left.

INTRANSIGENT (in-TRAN-zih-jint) *adj* — **stubborn; uncompromising**
Other forms: Intransigence *(noun)*; intransigently *(adv)*
Sentence: We tried to bargain with him, but he was *intransigent* in his price demands.

INTREPID (in-TREP-id) *adj* — **seemingly without fear; courageous**
Other form: Intrepidly *(adv);* intrepidness *(noun)*
Sentence: The first people on Mars will have to be *intrepid* explorers.

INTROSPECTION (in-tro-SPEK-shun) *noun* — **self-examination; looking within**
Other form: Introspect *(verb)*; introspective *(adj)*; introspectively *(adv)*
Sentence: Upon careful *introspection*, he realized he needed to change his attitude.

INUNDATE (IN-un-dayt) *verb* — **to flood; submerge; overwhelm**
Other forms: Inundation *(noun)*
Sentence: After the editorial, the newspaper was *inundated* with angry letters.

INURE (in-YOOR) *verb* — **become accustomed to; disciplined**
Other forms: Inured *(adj); inurement (noun)*
Sentence: After two years in Japan, he had become *inured* to its customs and culture.

INVALID (in-VAL-id) *adj* — **without foundation or legality; unacceptable**
Other forms: Invalidate *(verb);* invalidity *(noun);* invalidly *(adv)*
Sentence: Her card was *invalid* because she had not filled out the application correctly.

INVECTIVE (in-VEK-tiv) *noun* — **harsh words; verbal abuse**
Other forms: Invective *(adj);* invectively *(adv)*
Sentence: His angry sermon was filled with *invective* and accusation.

INVEIGH (in-VAY) *verb* — **to protest bitterly**
Sentence: Thousands stood in the streets and *inveighed* against the new law.

INVETERATE (in-VET-er-et) *adj* — **stubborn; persistent; chronic**
Other forms: Inveterately *(adv);* inveterateness *(noun)*
Sentence: He was an *inveterate* thief and had to be fired.

INVIDIOUS (in-VID-ee-uss) *adj* — **destructive; hateful**
Other forms: Invidiously *(adv);* invidiousness *(noun)*
Sentence: Public criticism, especially when *invidious*, can destroy morale.

INVINCIBLE (rep-ree-HEN-sih-bull) *adj* — **impossible to defeat, subdue, or overcome**
Other forms: Invincibility *(noun);* invincibly *(adv)*
Sentence: After thirty consecutive victories, the team seemed *invincible*.

INVIOLABLE (in-VY-uh-luh-bull) *adj* — **incapable of being infringed; incorruptible**
Other forms: Inviolableness *(noun);* inviolably *(adv);* inviolate *(adj)*
Sentence: It was an *inviolable* oath, one he would keep until the day he died.

IRATE (eye-RAYT) *adj* — **extremely angry; wrathful**
Other forms: Irately *(adv);* ire *(noun)*
Sentence: The mob was *irate* and eventually grew violent.

IRE (IRE) *noun* — **extreme anger**
    Other forms: Irate *(adj);* irately *(adv);* ire *(verb)*
    Sentence: His *ire* was raised every time his wife's family showed up unexpectedly.

IRIDESCENT (eer-ih-DESS-ent) *adj* — **shining with many colors; glittering**
    Other forms: Iridescence *(noun);* iridescently *(adv)*
    Sentence: The only color in the dark sky was an *iridescent* haze around the full moon.

IRKSOME (IRK-sum) *adj* — **irritating; annoying; tedious**
    Other forms: Irk *(verb);* irksomely *(adv);* irksomeness *(noun)*
    Sentence: His *irksome* habit of tapping his foot was driving her crazy.

IRREVOCABLE (ir-REV-uh-kuh-bull) *adj* — **incapable of being reversed or undone**
    Other forms: Irrevocability *(noun);* irrevocably *(adv)*
    Sentence: Once you press that delete key, the process is *irrevocable*: the file is gone.

ITINERANT (eye-TIN-er-ent) *adj* — **frequently going from one place to another**
    Other forms: Itinerancy *(noun);* itinerantly *(adv)*
    Sentence: We loved the *itinerant* lifestyle, always seeing new places.

ITINERARY (eye-TIN-uh-rer-ee) *noun* — **a plan or record of a trip; route**
    Sentence: Our *itinerary* included stops at all the major ports in the Mediterranean.

JOVIAL (JO-vee-ul) *adj* — **full of good humor; joyful; merry**
    Other forms: Joviality (noun); jovially *(adv)*
    Sentence: He was so *jovial* that he cheered everyone up in a matter of minutes.

JUBILATION (joo-bih-LAY-shun) *noun* — **visible expression of extreme joy; celebration**
    Other forms: Jubilant *(adj);* jubilantly *(adv)*
    Sentence: There was *jubilation* throughout the country after their team won.

JURISPRUDENCE (joor-is-PROO-dents) *noun* — **body of law; history of a judicial system**
    Other forms: Jurisprudent *(adj);* jurisprudentially *(adv)*
    Sentence: Even an expert in *jurisprudence* can't always predict a jury's verdict.

JUVENILE (JOO-veh-nyle) *adj* — **pertaining to children; immature**
　Other forms: Juvenile, juvenility (*nouns*)
　Sentence: I could tell by his *juvenile* behavior that he was still a child.

LABYRINTH (LAB-uh-rinth) *noun* — **a collection of interconnected passageways; maze**
　Other form: Labyrinthine (*adj*)
　Sentence: The building was a *labyrinth* of offices and hallways, and I was soon lost.

LABYRINTHINE (lab-uh-RIN-theen) *adj* — **complex; confusing**
　Other form: Labyrinth (*noun*)
　Sentence: The process to get a visitor's visa seemed *labyrinthine* and incomprehensibe.

LACERATION (lass-er-AY-shun) *noun* — **rough and jagged wound or piercing**
　Other forms: Lacerate (*verb*); lacerated (*adj*)
　Sentence: The man suffered severe *lacerations* when he was thrown from the car.

LACHRYMOSE (LAK-rih-mose) *adj* — **mournful; teary**
　Other forms: Lachrymosely (*adv*); lachrymosity (*noun*)
　Sentence: The eulogy was *lachrymose*, and by the end, everyone was crying.

LACKADAISICAL (lak-uh-DAYZ-ih-kull) *adj* — **lacking spirit or energy**
　Other form: Lackadaisically (*adv*)
　Sentence: It was a busy office, and my *lackadaisical* attitude wasn't appreciated.

LANGUID (LANG-wid) *adj* — **lacking energy or spirit; exhausted; lethargic**
　Other forms: Languidly (*adv*); languidness (*noun*)
　Sentence: I entered the marathon, but by the third mile my legs were *languid*.

LARCENY (LARSE-eh-nee) *noun* — **any act of illegally taking another's property**
　Other form: Larcenous (*adj*); larcenously (*adv*)
　Sentence: He was guilty of embezzlement, burglary, and other forms of *larceny*.

LARGESS (lar-JESS) *noun* — **gift or gratuity, usually given by a person of superior wealth or position**
　Other form: Largesse (*noun*)
　Sentence: He came to expect an annual *largess* from his wealthy grandfather.

72

LASSITUDE (LASS-ih-tood) *noun* — **idleness caused by either fatigue or lack of desire**
Sentence: He was driven by nothing but *lassitude*, lying in the grass for hours every day.

LAUDATORY (LAWD-uh-tor-ee) *adj* — **praising; worshipping**
Other forms: Laud *(verb);* laudable *(adj);* laudably *(adv)*
Sentence: We'd been expecting criticism, and were surprised by his *laudatory* remarks.

LAVISH (LAV-ish) *verb* — **to bestow in great abundance, sometimes wastefully**
Other forms: Lavish *(adj);* lavishly *(adv);* lavishness *(noun)*
Sentence: They *lavished* their son with so many toys, he needed a bigger room.

LENIENT (LEEN-yent) *adj* — **merciful; forgiving**
Other forms: Leniency *(noun);* leniently *(adv)*
Sentence: There were two judges at the courthouse: one *lenient*, the other merciless.

LETHARGY (LETH-er-jee) *noun* — **fatigue; chronic lack of energy**
Other forms: Lethargic *(adj);* lethargically *(adv)*
Sentence: My doctor said the medication could cause *lethargy*, and that I shouldn't drive.

LEVEE (LEV-ee) *noun* — **an embankment or wall designed to control floodwater**
Sentence: The *levee* couldn't withstand the hurricane's wind, and the city was flooded.

LIBEL (LY-bull) *verb* — **to defame another person, usually in print, without justification**
Other forms: Libel *(noun);* libelous *(adj);* libelously *(adv)*
Sentence: Tabloid newspapers are often sued for *libel* because of their unfounded claims.

LICENTIOUS (ly-SEN-shuss) *adj* — **lack of regard for morals or accepted behavior**
Other forms: Licentiously *(adv);* licentiousness *(noun)*
Sentence: The church denounced the film as being lewd and *licentious*.

LIEN (LEEN) *noun* — **a charge placed on personal property in order to satisfy a debt**
Sentence: The government threatened to put a *lien* on his house until the taxes were paid.

LIEU (LOO) *noun* — **stead; substitute**
    Sentence: She offered the landlord her diamond ring in *lieu* of the rent.

LIMPID (LIM-pid) *adj* — **clear; free of cloudiness; simple; peaceful**
    Other forms: Limpidly *(adv)*; limpidness *(noun)*
    Sentence: In the morning, you can look into the *limpid* lake and see the bottom.

LITHE (LYTH) *adj* — **agile; graceful; flexible**

    Other forms: Lithely *(adv)*; litheness *(noun)*; lithesome *(adj)*
    Sentence: The dancers' *lithe* bodies twisted in ways that seemed impossible.

LONGEVITY (long-jev-ih-tee) *noun* — **a long time, usually referring to a life**
    Sentence: His goal was *longevity*, so he never drank, smoked, or overate.

LUMINARY (LOO-min-err-ee) *noun* — **a successful person; or, a source of light**
    Sentence: All of the *luminaries* were in attendance at the awards ceremony.

LUMINOUS (LOO-min-uss) *adj* — **radiating bright light; shining; glowing**
    Other forms: Luminosity *(noun)*; luminously *(adv)*
    Sentence: The moon appears to be *luminous*, but it is just reflecting light from the sun.

LURID (LOOR-id) *adj* — **causing horror; hideous; ghastly**
    Other forms: Luridly *(adv)*; luridness *(noun)*
    Sentence: The green light gave everyone a *lurid* and deathly look.

LUSTROUS (LUSS-trus) *adj* — **shining; brilliant; radiant**
    Other forms: Luster *(noun)*; lustrously *(noun)*
    Sentence: Her face was *lustrous* with excitement.

MALADROIT (MAL-uh-droyt) *adj* — **lacking grace or dexterity; clumsy; awkward**
    Other forms: Maladroitly *(adv)*; maladroitness *(noun)*
    Sentence: I took one *maladroit* step onto the ice and I was flat on my back.

MALEVOLENCE (muh-LEV-uh-lents) *noun* — **vicious dislike toward another person**
    Other forms: Malevolent *(adj)*; malevolently *(adv)*; malice *(noun)*
    Sentence: His *malevolence* for his neighbor bordered on pure hatred.

MALINGER (muh-LING-er) *verb* — **to avoid work by pretending to be sick**
    Other form: Malingerer *(noun)*
    Sentence: He was a *malingering* employee, so we replaced him with a real worker.

MANDATE (MAN-dayt) *noun* — **order issued by a supreme authority**
    Other forms: Mandate *(verb)*; mandatorily *(adv)*; mandatory *(adj)*
    Sentence: The general received the president's *mandate* to attack.

MANDATORY (MAN-duh-tor-ee) *adj* — **required; obligatory**
    Other forms: Mandate *(verb)*; mandatorily *(adv)*
    Sentence: At first we thought participation was voluntary, only to learn it was *mandatory*.

MANIFEST (MAN-ih-fest) *adj* — **readily perceived; evident; obvious**
    Other forms: Manifest *(verb)*; manifest, manifestation *(nouns)*
    Sentence: The skydiving student said he was ready to jump, but his fear was *manifest*.

MASSACRE (MASS-uh-ker) *verb* — **to brutally murder, especially in large numbers**
    Other form: Massacre *(noun)*
    Sentence: It is astonishing how many rulers choose to *massacre* their own people.

MAUDLIN (MAUD-lin) *adj* — **excessively weepy or sentimental**
    Sentence: His *maudlin* toast of the bride and groom depressed everyone at the wedding.

MAVERICK (MAV-er-ik) *noun* — **group member who strays from customary practices**
    Other forms: Maverick *(adj)*
    Sentence: A *maverick* who refuses to conform will have a difficult time in the military.

MAWKISH (MAW-kish) *adj* — **insincerely or overly sentimental**
    Other forms: Mawkishly *(adv)*; mawkishness *(noun)*
    Sentence: All that *mawkish* hugging, and then she insults you behind your back.

MAXIM (MAX-im) *noun* — **a general truth or rule; axiom**
Sentence: She had a ready *maxim* on hand for every possible situation.

MEDIATE (MEED-ee-ayt) *verb* — **negotiate a settlement; bring opposing parties together**
Other forms: Mediation, mediator *(nouns)*
Sentence: They just couldn't agree, and had to hire someone to *mediate* the issue.

MEDLEY (MED-lee) *noun* — **a mixture of generally unlike items**
Sentence: She performed a *medley* of songs that really showed off her versatility.

MENDACIOUS (men-DAY-shuss) *adj* — **deceiving; dishonest**
Other forms: Mendaciously *(adv);* mendacity *(noun)*
Sentence: His claim to have never lied was just one more of his *mendacious* statements.

MENDICANT (MEN-dih-kent) *noun* — **beggar**
Other form: Mendicant (adj)
Sentence: He was a *mendicant*, but had dreams of someday earning a good living.

MERCENARY (MER-suh-ner-ee) *noun* — **person, often a soldier, paid for his work**
Other form: Mercenary *(adj)*
Sentence: Many knights during the Middle Ages were *mercenaries*, paid to fight.

MERCURIAL (mer-KYOOR-ee-el) *adj* — **tending to change quickly and unpredictably**
Other forms: Mercurially *(adv)*
Sentence: My aunt had a *mercurial* nature: laughing one minute, angry the next.

MERETRICIOUS (mer-uh-TRISH-uss) *adj* — **synthetically attractive; insincere; gaudy**
Other forms: Meretriciously *(adv);* meretriciousness *(noun)*
Sentence: The car had a *meretricious* beauty, but was actually a piece of junk.

MESMERIZE (MEZ-mer-ize) *verb* — **to hold spellbound; enthrall; hypnotize**
Other forms: Mesmerism *(noun)*; mesmerizing *(adj)*
Sentence: We were *mesmerized* by the beautiful sunset.

METAMORPHOSIS (met-uh-MOR-fuh-sis) *noun* — **a dramatic change in form**
Other forms: Metamorphic *(adj);* metamorphose *(verb)*
Sentence: His *metamorphosis* from skinny boy to muscular man was startling.

METTLE (MET-ul) *noun* — **characteristics of strength, especially those needed in a given situation**
Sentence: Her attempt to sail around the world would surely test her *mettle.*

METTLESOME (MET-ul-sum) *adj* — **high-spirited**
Sentence: The actor got a standing ovation for his *mettlesome* performance.

MILIEU (mill-YOO) *noun* — **setting; environment**
Sentence: The *milieu* of this novel is 17th Century Spain.

MIMIC (MIM-ik) *verb* — **to copy or imitate, sometimes in order to ridicule**
Other forms: Mimic, mimicry *(nouns)*
Sentence: He could *mimic* the teacher down to the most subtle gestures.

MISANTHROPE (MISS-an-thrope) *noun* — **one who hates all people**
Other form: Misanthropic *(adj)*
Sentence: He was more than a racist; he was a *misanthrope,* and hated everyone.

MISCHIEVOUS (MISS-chuh-vuss) *adj* — **tending to cause trouble; annoying**
Other forms: Mischief *(adj);* mischievously *(adv)*
Sentence: He had been *mischievous* as a boy, but grew into a law-abiding citizen.

MISER (MY-zer) *noun* — **person who lives as if in poverty in order to keep his money**
Other forms: Miserliness *(noun)*; miserly *(adv)*
Sentence: Our neighbor was a *miser* who never spent a penny on anyone.

MISOGYNIST (miss-OJ-ih-nist) *noun* — **one who hates women**
Other form: Misogyny *(noun)*
Sentence: Not surprisingly, the person who killed all those women was a *misogynist.*

MITE (MITE) *noun* — **an extremely small amount**
    Sentence: I wasn't hungry, so I asked for just a *mite* of bread.

MODERATION (mod-er-AY-shun) *noun* — **in controlled and sensible amounts**
    Other form: Moderate *(adj)*; moderate *(verb)*; moderately *(adv)*
    Sentence: If you eat in *moderation* and get some exercise, you can stay in shape.

MODICUM (MOD-ih-kum) *noun* — **a very small amount; extremely low level**
    Sentence: The tragedy left him without a *modicum* of dignity.

MOLT (MOLT) *verb* — **to shed an outing covering; discard**
    Other form: Molt *(noun)*
    Sentence: Many animals *molt*, shedding their heavy fur or feathers after winter.

MOMENTOUS (mo-MEN-tuss) *adj* — **greatly important**
    Other form: Moment *(noun)*
    Sentence: The first moon landing was a *momentous* occasion for scientists everywhere.

MONOTONOUS (muh-NOT-uh-nus) *adj* — **having no change in sound; repetitious**
    Other forms: Monotone, monotony *(nouns)*; monotonously *(adv)*
    Sentence: A *monotonous* speaker can put an audience to sleep.

MORATORIUM (mor-uh-TOR-ee-um) *noun* — **delay or suspension of some usual activity**
    Sentence: The company announced a *moratorium* on all raises until business improved.

MORBID (MOR-bid) *adj* — **related to disease or death; gloomy**
    Other forms: Morbidity *(noun)*; morbidly *(adv)*
    Sentence: *Morbid* stories about your childhood will not make us feel better about ours.

MORIBUND (MOR-ih-bund) *adj* — **near death; showing little life**
    Other form: Moribundity *(noun)*
    Sentence: This show is *moribund*, and needs someone to inject new life into it.

MULTIFARIOUS (mul-tih-FAIR-ee-uss) *adj* — **having great variety; diverse**
Other forms: Multifariously *(adv);* multifariousness *(noun)*
Sentence: His activities were so *multifarious*, it was hard even for him to keep track.

MUNIFICENCE (myoo-NIF-uh-sents) *noun* — **extreme generosity**
Other forms: Munificent *(noun);* munificently *(adv)*
Sentence: Successful business people are often most remembered for their *munificence.*

MUNIFICENT (myoo-NIF-uh-sent) *adj* — **giving freely and in great abundance**
Other form: Munificence *(noun);* munificently *(adv)*
Sentence: You are a *munificent* and kind member of this community.

NADIR (NAY-der) *noun* — **the lowest point**
Sentence: At the *nadir* of her career, she was still one of the world's most famous people.

NASCENT (NAY-shent) *adj* — **in the earliest stages of existence or life**
Other form: Nascence *(noun)*
Sentence: Astronomers try to imagine what the *nascent* universe was like.

NEBULOUS (NEB-yoo-lus) *adj* — **not clearly defined; vague; hazy**
Other forms: Nebulosity *(noun);* nebulously *(adv)*
Sentence: You can't expect funding based on such a *nebulous* and undeveloped idea.

NECROLOGY (nuh-KRAHL-uh-jee) *noun* — **a record of deaths; obituaries**
Other form: Necrological *(adj)*
Sentence: It's difficult to get a complete *necrology* of those killed in a major disaster.

NEGATE (nuh-GAYT) *verb* — **to deny the validity of; to nullify**
Other forms: Negation *(noun);* negative *(adj);* negatively *(adv)*
Sentence: A single criminal act can *negate* a lifetime of good works.

NEMESIS (NEM-uh-sis) *noun* — **an opponent, usually one in a long-running conflict**
Sentence: He was about to step into the ring and face his old *nemesis* once again.

NOISOME (NOY-sum) *adj* — **destructive; noxious; unwholesome**
    Other forms: Noisomely *(adv)*; noisomeness *(noun)*
    Sentence: Toxic waste can create a *noisome* environment far from its source.

NOMADIC (no-MAD-ik) *adj* — **wandering; without a permanent home**
    Other forms: Nomad *(noun)*
    Sentence: Members of *nomadic* tribes usually carry their homes on their backs.

NOMINAL (NAH-min-ul) *adj* — **existing in name only; insignificant**
    Other form: Nominally *(adv)*
    Sentence: Your jewelry has *nominal* value, if any at all.

NONCHALANT (non-shuh-LANT) *adj* — **lack of concern; unruffled**
    Other forms: Nonchalance *(noun)*; nonchalantly *(adv)*
    Sentence: She seemed *nonchalant*, considering she was about to climb an active volcano.

NONDESCRIPT (non-duh-SKRIPT) *adj* — **lacking distinction; not classifiable**
    Other form: Nondescript *(noun)*
    Sentence: Trying to blend in, he wore plain clothes and drove a *nondescript* car.

NOSTRUM (NOSS-trum) *noun* — **a cure-all; a dubious scheme or remedy**
    Sentence: His specialty was natural cures, and he had a *nostrum* for every ailment.

NOTORIETY (no-tuh-RY-uh-tee) *noun* — **fame, usually based on a negative reputation**
    Other forms: Notorious *(adj)*; notoriously *(adv)*
    Sentence: Many bank robbers achieved *notoriety*, and some were treated as celebrities.

NOVICE (NAH-viss) *noun* — **one who is inexperienced; neophyte**
    Sentence: She could tell I was a *novice* at chess, and went easy on me.

NOXIOUS (NOK-shuss) *adj* — **harmful; destructive; pernicious**
    Other forms: Noxiously *(adv)*; noxiousness *(noun)*
    Sentence: One person with a bad attitude can have a *noxious* effect on an entire staff.

NUGATORY (NOO-guh-tor-ee) *adj* — **having no value; worthless; insignificant**
    Other forms: Nugacity, nugation *(nouns)*
    Sentence: In that remote land, we realized our money and jewels were *nugatory* trifles.

OBFUSCATE (OB-fus-kayt) *verb* — **to make confusing or unclear; to obscure**
    Other forms: Obfuscated *(adj);* obfuscation *(noun)*
    Sentence: He had something to hide and was trying to *obfuscate* the truth.

OBLIQUE (oh-BLEEK) *adj* — **not straightforward; at an angle; obscure**
    Other forms: Obliquely *(adv);* obliqueness *(noun)*
    Sentence: The prosecutor's question was *oblique*, not directly confronting the witness.

OBLIVION (uh-BLIV-ee-yon) *noun* — **the state of forgetfulness, or having been forgotten**
    Other forms: Oblivious *(adj);* obliviously *(adv)*
    Sentence: After years of fame she retired into *oblivion*, never to be heard from again.

OBLIVIOUS (uh-BLIV-ee-yuss) *adj* — **forgetful; unaware**
    Other forms: Oblivion *(noun);* obliviously *(adv)*
    Sentence: He was *oblivious* of the police siren and kept driving through the roadblock.

OBSTREPEROUS (ob-STREP-er-uss) *adj* — **noisy; rebellious; unmanageable**
    Other form:s Obstreperously *(adv);* obstreperousness *(noun)*
    Sentence: Worn out by her children's *obstreperousness*, she fled to the quiet bedroom.

OBTRUSIVE (ob-TROO-siv) *adj* — **pushing into sight; attention-grabbing**
    Other forms: Obtrude *(verb);* obtrusively *(adv);* obtrusiveness *(noun)*
    Sentence: The yellow barn was so *obtrusive*, it spoiled the rest of the view.

ODIOUS (OH-dee-uss) *adj* — **deserving to be loathed; hateful**
    Other forms: Odiously *(adv);* odium *(noun)*
    Sentence: The gang's *odious* behavior disgusted everyone who heard about it.

ODIUM (OH-dee-um) *noun* — **hatred; dishonor; comdemnation**
    Other forms: Odious *(adj);* odiously *(adv)*
    Sentence: He risked the community's *odium* and confessed to the crime.

OFFICIOUS (oh-FISH-us) *adj* — **meddlesome; intrusive; impertinent**
Other forms: Officiously *(adv);* officiousness *(noun)*
Sentence: She said she was trying to be helpful, but I found her to be *officious* and rude.

OLFACTORY (ole-FAK-tuh-ree) *adj* — **having to do with the sense of smell**
Other form: Olfactorily *(adv)*
Sentence: The *olfactory* stimulus evoked a flood of memories.

ONUS (OH-nus) *noun* — **difficult or distasteful task; burden; blame**
Sentence: Trying to avoid responsibility, he placed the *onus* on the rest of the group.

OPULENT (OPP-yoo-lent) *adj* — **wealthy; luxurious**
Other forms: Opulence *(noun);* opulently *(adv)*
Sentence: A grand staircase was one of the symbols of an *opulent* mansion.

ORATION (awr-AY-shun) *noun* — **a long speech, usually intended to instruct**
Other forms: Orate *(verb)*; oratorical *(adj)*; oratorically *(adv)*; oratory *(noun)*
Sentence: We were expecting a quick comment, but were subjected to an *oration.*

ORNATE (or-NAYT) *adj* — **intricately decorative; embellished**
Other forms: Ornament *(noun)*; ornately *(adv)*
Sentence: The wooden box was decorated with elaborately *ornate* carvings.

ORTHODOX (OR-thuh-doks) *adj* — **traditional; conventional; conservative**
Other form: Orthodoxy *(noun)*
Sentence: Her family belonged to an *orthodox* religion, with strict dietary rules.

OSCILLATE (OSS-ih-layt) *verb* — **to swing back and forth at regular intervals**
Other form: Oscillating *(adj)*; oscillation *(noun)*
Sentence: The engine moves an *oscillating* arm, which turns the wheels.

OSSIFY (OSS-ih-fye) *verb* — **to turn to bone; to harden or become rigid**
Other form: Ossification *(noun)*
Sentence: Our once dynamic group has *ossified* into an inflexible mass.

OSTENSIBLE (ah-STEN-sih-bull) *adj* — **capable of being shown; apparent**
Other forms: Ostensibly *(adv)*; ostensive *(adj)*
Sentence: The *ostensible* reason for her visit was that she missed us; we knew better.

OSTENTATIOUS (ah-sten-TAY-shuss) *adj* — **overly elaborate; frilly; gaudy**
Other forms: Ostentation *(noun)*; ostentatiously *(adv)*
Sentence: The party was so *ostentatious*, it must have cost a fortune.

OSTRACIZE (OSS-truh-size) *verb* — **to banish from a group; to alienate**
Other form: Ostracism *(noun)*
Sentence: A teenager can be *ostracized* simply for wearing the wrong kind of jeans.

PALATE (PAL-et) *noun* — **the roof of the mouth; an individual's sense of taste**
Other forms: Palatable *(adj)*; palatably *(adv)*
Sentence: Most people find sweets pleasing to the *palate*.

PALATIAL (puh-LAY-shul) *adj* — **like a palace; grand; magnificent**
Other forms: Palatially *(adv)*; palatialness *(noun)*
Sentence: We were accustomed to a small cottage, so their house seemed *palatial*.

PALETTE (PAL-et) *noun* — **an oval board for holding an artist's paint; range of colors**
Sentence: We immediately recognized the artist by her *palette*.

PALLIATE (PAL-ee-ayt) *verb* — **to ease pain or discomfort; soothe**
Other forms: Palliation *(noun)*; palliative *(adj)*
Sentence: His doctor prescribed drugs strictly for *palliative* care; there was no cure.

PALLID (PAL-id) *adj* — **lacking color or sparkle; dull; wan**
Other forms: Pallidly *(adv)*; pallidness *(noun)*
Sentence: We could tell by her *pallid* complexion that she hadn't left the house in weeks.

PALPABLE (PALP-uh-bull) *adj* — **capable of being felt; perceptible; evident**
Other form: Palpability *(noun)*; palpably *(adv)*
Sentence: Just before the storm, there was a *palpable* feeling of electricity in the air.

PANACEA (pan-uh-SEE-uh) *noun* — **universal remedy; cure-all**
　　Other form: Panacean *(adj)*
　　Sentence: Money is not a *panacea* for the shortcomings of the educational system.

PANDEMONIUM (pan-deh-MO-nee-um) *noun* — **uncontrollable uproar; chaos**
　　Other form: Pandemoniac *(adj)*
　　Sentence: If there were a need to evacuate quickly, there would be *pandemonium*.

PANEGYRIC (pan-uh-JEER-ik) *noun* — **a speech or letter filled with praise**
　　Other forms: Panegyrical *(adj)*; panegyrically *(adv)*; panegyrize *(verb)*
　　Sentence: His speech at the funeral was a *panegyric* about a well-spent life.

PARADIGM (PAR-uh-dime) *noun* — **philosophical structure or pattern; set of beliefs**
　　Other form: Paradigmatic *(adj)*
　　Sentence: Einstein's theories ushered in a new *paradigm* in physics.

PARADOX (PAR-uh-doks) *noun* — **seemingly true statements that are contradictory**
　　Other forms: Paradoxical *(adj);* paradoxically *(adv)*
　　Sentence: This *paradox* has puzzled mathematicians for centuries.

PARAMOUNT (PAR-uh-mount) *adj* — **superior; most important; overriding**
　　Other form: Paramountly *(adv)*
　　Sentence: In any building design, the safety of the occupants is *paramount*.

PARIAH (puh-RY-uh) *noun* — **person rejected by his own people; outcast**
　　Sentence: Once a hero, he was now treated as a *pariah*, shunned by everyone.

PARLEY (PAR-lee) *noun* — **discussion; meeting; conference**
　　Other form: Parley *(verb)*
　　Sentence: The *parley* ended with no real agreement being reached.

PARODY (PAR-uh-dee) *verb* — **to imitate for comic effect; to caricature**
　　Other form: Parody *(noun)*
　　Sentence: Their attempt to *parody* the movie fell flat, as no one had seen the original.

PATENT (PAY-tent) *adj* — **clear; obvious; evident**
Other form: Patently *(adv)*
Sentence: Their winning that contract is a *patent* example of corruption.

PATHOS (PAY-thos) *noun* — **that which evokes grief, pity, or compassion**
Sentence: We saw a play that was filled with *pathos*, yet was also funny at times.

PATRIARCH (PAY-tree-ark) *noun* — **The male head of a family, community, or religion**
Other forms: Patriarchal, patriarchic *(adj)*; patriarchy *(noun)*
Sentence: He was the *patriarch*, so most major family decisions came from him.

PATRICIAN (puh-TRISH-un) *noun* — **member of a high class in society; aristocrat**
Other forms: Patrician *(adj)*; patricianly *(adv)*
Sentence: She moved like a *patrician*, seemingly waiting to be served at every turn.

PATRONIZE (PAY-truh-nyz) *verb* — **to support; also, to treat as an inferior**
Other form: Patronization *(noun)*; patronizing *(adj)*
Sentence: He resented the way she *patronized* him, as though he were a child.

PECCADILLO (pek-uh-DILL-oh) *noun* — **a slight offense; minor indiscretion**
Sentence: A *peccadillo* here and there did little to tarnish his golden reputation.

PEDANTIC (puh-DAN-tik) *adj* — **having a tendency to show off one's learning**
Other forms: Pedant, pedantry *(nouns)*; pedantically *(adv)*
Sentence: His *pedantic* lectures did little to inspire, teach, or impress.

PEDESTRIAN (puh-DESS-tree-en) *adj* — **unimaginative; common; dull**
Sentence: An experienced publisher can quickly spot and reject a *pedestrian* manuscript.

PEJORATIVE (puh-JAR-uh-tiv) *adj* — **making less or worse; demeaning; disparaging**
Other forms: Pejorative *(noun)*; pejoratively *(adv)*
Sentence: Your *pejorative* remarks about them don't reflect well on your character.

PELLUCID (peh-LOOS-id) *adj* — **perfectly clear; readily understood**
Other forms: Pellucidly *(adv);* pellucidness *(noun)*
Sentence: I've always found chemistry confusing, but his *pellucid* explanations helped.

PENITENT (PEN-ih-tent) *adj* — **sorry for past sins and offenses; remorseful**
Other forms: Penitence *(noun)*; penitential *(adj)*; penitently *(adv)*
Sentence: He seemed *penitent*, but the jury could not overlook the severity of his crimes.

PENULTIMATE (pen-UL-tih-mit) *adj* — **next to the last**
Other form: Penultimate *(noun);* penultimately *(adv)*
Sentence: On the *penultimate* day of their trip, they decided to move there permanently.

PEREMPTORY (per-EMP-ter-ee) *adj* — **decisive; confident; resolute**
Other forms: Peremptorily *(adv);* peremptoriness *(noun)*
Sentence: Her *peremptory* opening remarks immediately prevented any objection.

PERFIDY (PER-fih-dee) *noun* — **disloyalty; betrayal**
Other form: Perfidious *(adj)*; perfidiously *(adv)*; perfidiousness *(noun)*
Sentence: The reward for your chronic *perfidy* is that no one trusts or believes you.

PERIPATETIC (per-uh-puh-TET-ik) *adj* — **moving from place to place; itinerant**
Other form: Peripatetically *(adv)*
Sentence: They were *peripatetic* travelers, never staying in one place very long.

PERJURE (PER-jer) *verb* — **to lie under oath**
Other forms: Perjurious *(adj);* perjury *(noun)*
Sentence: If you *perjure* yourself, you could go to prison for many years.

PERJURY (PER-jer-ee) *noun* — **lying under oath**
Other forms: Perjure *(verb);* perjurious *(adj)*
Sentence: The punishment for *perjury* can be harsher than the action you lied about.

PERMEATE (PER-me-ayt) *verb* — **to pass into, as a liquid through the pores of a fabric**
Other forms: Permeability *(noun)*; permeable *(adj)*; permeably *(adv)*
Sentence: The motivational speaker tried to get his positive ideas to *permeate* our minds.

PERQUISITE (PERK-wiz-it) *noun* — **fringe benefit associated with a job or position**
Sentence: One of the most coveted *perquisites* at my job is an assigned parking space.

PERSEVERE (per-suh-VEER) *verb* — **to continue, even under adverse conditions; persist**
Other forms: Perseverence *(noun)*; persevering *(adj)*
Sentence: Most success comes after you *persevere* through many failures.

PERSIFLAGE (PERS-uh-flazh) *noun* — **light banter, usually derisive**
Other form: Persiflate *(verb)*
Sentence: She wasn't used to being kidded, so our *persiflage* seemed cruel to her.

PERSONABLE (PER-son-uh-bull) *adj* — **pleasing in appearance**
Other form: Personability *(noun)*
Sentence: Her looks and personality made her the most *personable* of the applicants.

PERTINACIOUS (per-tin-AY-shuss) *adj* — **stubborn; persistent; unrelenting**
Other forms: Pertinaciously *(adv)*; pertinacity *(noun)*
Sentence: He was so *pertinacious* about getting a raise that I agreed just to shut him up.

PERTINENT (PER-tin-ent) *adj* — **relevant; applicable; related**
Other forms: Pertinence *(noun)*; pertinently *(adv)*
Sentence: She brought up a point that was slightly off-topic, but still *pertinent*.

PERTURB (per-TURB) *verb* — **to bother; upset; agitate**
Other forms: Perturbation *(noun)*; perturbed *(adj)*
Sentence: After three interruptions, the speaker was *perturbed* and refused to continue.

PETRIFY (PETCH-rih-fy) *verb* — **to cause to harden into stone; also, to paralyze**
Other form: Petrification *(noun)*; petrified *(adj)*
Sentence: A *petrified* tree can yield a lot of information to scientists.

PETULANT (PEH-choo-lent) *adj* — **rude; irritable; peevish**
Other forms: Petulance *(noun)*; petulantly *(adv)*
Sentence: My daughter is being *petulant*, and nothing will make her happy right now.

PHENOMENON (fuh-NOM-ih-non) *noun* — **an observable event; a real experience**
    Other form: Phenomenal *(adj)*
    Sentence: Was that a natural *phenomenon*, or something unexplainable?

PHILANTHROPIC (fil-an-THROP-ik) *adj* — **engaged in acts of good will or charity**
    Other forms: Philanthropically *(adv);* philanthropist, philanthropy *(nouns)*
    Sentence: They enjoyed their wealth, but were also *philanthropic*, giving to the needy.

PHILANTHROPY (fil-AN-thro-pee) *noun* — **to practice of helping others, especially by donating time or money**
    Other forms: Philanthropic *(adj)* philanthropically *(adv);* philanthropist
    Sentence: This hospital wouldn't be here were it not for the *philanthropy* of good people.

PHILISTINE (FIL-ih-steen) *adj* — **insensitive; aesthetically ignorant**
    Other form: Philistine *(noun)*
    Sentence: Their *philistine* attitude toward the museum was the cause of its demise.

PICARESQUE (PIK-uh-resk) *adj* — **characteristic of rascals; roguish**
    Other form: Picaresque *(noun)*
    Sentence: The image of *picaresque* orphans preying on tourists is not accurate.

PILLAGE (PILL-ij) *verb* — **the act of stealing, especially from those conquered in war**
    Other form: Pillage *(noun)*
    Sentence: After *pillaging* each town, the soldiers burned down the buildings.

PINNACLE (PIN-uh-kull) *noun* — **highest point; peak; ultimate achievement**
    Sentence: Few athletes can retire while still at the *pinnacle* of their careers.

PIQUE (PEEK) *verb* — **to irritate; to arouse an emotion**
    Other form: Pique *(noun)*
    Sentence: A good writer will try to *pique* the reader's interest on page one.

PITTANCE (PIT-ince) *noun* — **a very small amount that is barely enough**
    Sentence: It was hard for the workers to get by on the *pittance* they were paid.

PIVOTAL (PIV-uh-tull) *adj* — **critically important; affecting all other components**
Other forms: Pivot *(noun)*; pivot *(verb)*; pivotally *(adv)*
Sentence: Your cooperation was *pivotal*: the project would have failed without you.

PLACID (PLASS-id) *adj* — **calm; peaceful; serene**
Other forms: Placidly *(adv)*; placidity *(noun)*
Sentence: We had been enjoying the *placid* lake when a motorboat roared by.

PLAINTIVE (PLAYN-tiv) *adj* — **full of suffering or sorrow; melancholy**
Other forms: Plaintively *(adv)*; plaintiveness *(noun)*
Sentence: I could hear the *plaintive* cry of the elephant as she mourned the loss of a calf.

PLAUDIT (PLAW-dit) *noun* — **enthusiastic praise; applause**
Other forms: Plaudit *(verb)*; plauditory *(adj)*
Sentence: As an artist, the *plaudits* of the critics were all the pay he needed right now.

PLEA (PLEE) *noun* — **answer to a legal charge; a fervent request**
Other form: Plead *(verb)*
Sentence: Rescuers could hear his *plea* for help.

PLENITUDE (PLEN-ih-tood *noun* — **fullness; completeness; abundance**
Other form: Plenitudinous *(adj)*
Sentence: Her office was a *plenitude* of books and papers, leaving no room to walk.

PLETHORA (PLETH-er-uh) *noun* — **an overflow; excess; superfluity**
Other form: Plethoric *(adj)*
Sentence: We received such a *plethora* of letters, it was impossible to read them all.

PLIABLE (PLY-uh-bull) *adj* — **flexible; bendable; supple**
Other forms: Pliability *(noun)*; pliably *(adv)*
Sentence: After the sun warmed it, the hose became *pliable* again.

PLUMB (PLUM) *verb* — **to examine or test to a great depth**
Other forms: Plumb *(noun)*; plumb *(adj)*
Sentence: His correspondence forced her to *plumb* the depths of her feelings.

PLUMMET (PLUM-it) *verb* — **to fall straight down, quickly and a great distance**
    Other form: Plummeting *(adj)*
    Sentence: The goose, hit with a single gunshot, *plummeted* to the ground

POIGNANT (POYN-yent) *adj* — **emotionally touching; keenly affecting**
    Other forms: Poignancy *(noun);* poignantly *(adv)*
    Sentence: The scene in which the boy leaves is both *poignant* and hopeful.

POLEMIC (puh-LEM-ik) *noun* — **a sharply aggressive verbal attack; rant**
    Other forms: Polemical *(adj);* polemically *(adv)*
    Sentence: Her *polemic* on the evils of communism are still quoted worldwide.

POLYGLOT (POL-ee-glot) *noun* — **a mixture of different languages**
    Other forms: Polyglot, polyglotal *(adj)*
    Sentence: Walk the streets of most big cities and you will hear a *polyglot* of speech.

POMMEL (POMM-el) *noun* — **a knob or protuberance, usually ornamental**
    Sentence: The sword had a carved *pommel* on either side of the hilt.

PORTEND (por-TEND) *verb* — **to predict; foreshadow; forecast**
    Other forms: Portent *(noun)*; portentious *(adj);* portentiously *(adv)*
    Sentence: Not that long ago, a comet was thought to *portend* a coming catastrophe.

POTENTATE (POTE-en-tayt) *noun* — **ruler who wields great power; dictator**
    Other form: Potent *(adj)*
    Sentence: One *potentate* might be caring and protective, the next ruthless.

PRAGMATIC (prag-MAT-ik) *adj* — **relating to practical matters; using common sense**
    Other form: Pragmatically *(adv)*; pragmatism *(noun)*
    Sentence: His *pragmatic* approach made traveling predictable, but not very exciting.

PRECEDENT (PRESS-ih-dent) *noun* — **one that came before and had a subsequent effect**
    Other forms: Precede *(verb)*; precedence *(noun)*
    Sentence: She could find no *precedent* in history; perhaps it had never happened before.

PRECIPICE (PRESS-ih-pis) *noun* — **face of a steep cliff; very dangerous situation**
Other forms: Precipitous *(adj);* precipitously *(adv)*
Sentence: The car stopped at the edge of the *precipice* before plunging over.

PRECIPITATE (pre-SIP-ih-tayt) *verb* — **to cause to happen; to press**
Other form: Precipitation *(noun);* precipitative *(adj)*
Sentence: He thought the question harmless, but it *precipitated* a long and bitter debate.

PRECIPITOUS (pre-SIP-ih-tuss) *adj* — **marked by haste and lack of caution; impulsive**
Other forms: Precipice *(noun);* precipitously *(adv)*
Sentence: She found herself in a *precipitous* situation, and didn't know what to do.

PRECURSOR (PRE-ker-ser) *noun* — **one that comes before in an evolutionary process**
Other form: Precursory *(adj)*
Sentence: It seems likely that a burnt stick was a *precursor* to the pencil.

PREDICAMENT (pruh-DIK-uh-ment) *noun* — **difficult position; dilemma**
Sentence: He frantically wondered how he'd get out of this *predicament*.

PREDOMINATE (pre-DOM-in-ayt) *verb* — **to be in control; govern; rule**
Other forms: Predominance *(noun);* predominant *(adj);* predominantly *(adv)*
Sentence: Hungry for power, he wanted no less than to *predominate* the continent.

PREMATURE (pre-mah-CHOOR) *adj* — **happening too soon**
Other forms: Prematurely *(adv);* prematurity *(noun)*
Sentence: The runners' start was *premature*, and everyone had to go back.

PREPONDERANCE (pruh-PON-der-ents) *noun* — **an excess in number or weight**
Other forms: Preponderant *(adj);* preponderantly *(adv)*
Sentence: A *preponderance* of the evidence proved them guilty.

PREROGATIVE (pre-ROG-uh-tiv) *noun* — **an ability to decide based on rank or position**
Other form: Prerogative *(adj)*
Sentence: It was her *prerogative*, and we had to respect her decision.

PRESAGE (pre-SAGE) *verb* — **to predict or warn of a future event, usually unpleasant**
Other forms: Presage *(noun)*; presaging *(adj)*; presagingly *(adv)*
Sentence: A lunar eclipse was thought to *presage* death and destruction.

PRESCIENT (PRESH-ent) *adj* — **inexplicably having knowledge beforehand**
Other forms: Prescience *(noun)*; presciently *(adv)*
Sentence: My grandmother believed dreams give a *prescient* look into the future.

PRESUMPTION (pre-ZUMP-shun) *noun* — **an assumption, perhaps based on evidence**
Other forms: Presume *(verb)*; presumptive *(adj)*
Sentence: There is a *presumption* of innocence until the accused is proved guilty.

PRESUMPTUOUS (pre-ZUMP-choo-uss) *adj* — **assuming privileges; taking liberties**
Other forms: Presumptuously *(adv)*; presumptuousness *(noun)*
Sentence: It was *presumptuous* of you to come over uninvited.

PRETERNATURAL (preet-er-NATCH-er-ull) *adj* — **abnormal; supernatural**
Other form: Preternaturally *(adv)*
Sentence: Many people think crop circles are *preternatural* events, not caused by humans.

PREVARICATE (pre-VAR-ih-kayt) *verb* — **to speak evasively or dishonestly; to lie**
Other form: Prevarication *(noun)*; prevaricative *(adj)*
Sentence: He continued to *prevaricate* when all she wanted was a straight answer.

PRIM (PRIM) *adj* — **in a precise manner; formal**
Other forms: Prim *(verb)*; primly *(adv)*
Sentence: Her *prim* manner and approach gave away her private school training.

PRIMEVAL (pri-MEE-vul) *adj* — **dating back to the earliest period in Earth's past**
Other form: Primevally *(adv)*
Sentence: We found ourselves in a *primeval* forest, ancient and untouched.

PRISTINE (priss-TEEN) *adj* — **pure; uncorrupted; immaculate**
Other form: Pristinely *(adv)*
Sentence: The *pristine* condition of the manuscript made it that much more valuable.

PROBITY (PRO-bih-tee) *noun* — **an unwavering adherence to high standards**
Sentence: His unyielding *probity*, in the face of unreasonable demands, was admirable.

PROCLIVITY (pro-KLIV-ih-tee) *noun* — **a strong tendency; leaning**
Sentence: Both of our parents were doctors, so we had a *proclivity* toward science.

PROCRASTINATE (pro-KRASS-tin-ayt) *verb* — **to habitually put off doing something that should be done; delay**
Other form: Procrastination *(noun)*
Sentence: Imagine how much more he could have done if he didn't *procrastinate*.

PROFANE (pro-FAYN) *adj* — **disrespectful, especially of the sacred; vulgar**
Other forms: Profanely *(adv);* profanity *(noun)*
Sentence: The story was well-told, but we found the *profane* language bothersome.

PROFLIGATE (PROF-lih-git) *adj* — **uncontrollably wasteful**
Other forms: Profligacy *(noun)*; profligately *(adv)*
Sentence: Your *profligate* ways will leave you penniless.

PROFUNDITY (pro-FUN-dih-tee) *noun* — **deeply meaningful idea or statement**
Other forms: Profound *(adj);* profoundly *(adv)*
Sentence: Our professor was a fountain of *profundity*, and we wrote down his every word.

PROLETARIAT (pro-leh-TAIR-ee-at) *noun* — **member of a society's working class**
Other form: Proletarian *(adj)*
Sentence: The *proletariat* discontent was beginning to rumble toward revolt.

PROLIFIC (pro-LIF-ik) *adj* — **highly productive; fertile; abundant**
Other forms: Proliferation *(noun)*; prolifically *(adv)*
Sentence: She was a *prolific* author, writing an average of two books every year.

PROLIX (PRO-lix) *adj* — **wordy; long-winded; repetitious**
Other forms: Prolixity *(noun)*; prolixly *(adv)*
Sentence: Your essay was well-written, but *prolix*; please be more concise.

PROMULGATE (PROM-ul-gayt) *verb* — **to make known; to declare**
Other form: Promulgation *(noun)*
Sentence: He traveled the countryside, *promulgating* his newly-adopted religious beliefs.

PROPAGATE (PROP-uh-gayt) *verb* — **to cause to continue or flourish; to spread**
Other forms: Propagation *(adv);* propagative *(adj)*
Sentence: Although not native to the island, the plant *propagated* quickly in the rich soil.

PROPENSITY (pro-PEN-sih-tee) *noun* — **tendency; proclivity**
Sentence: His *propensity* for gambling had turned into an addiction.

PROPITIOUS (pro-PISH-uss) *adj* — **providing a favorable outlook; encouraging**
Other forms: Propitiously *(adv);* propitiousness *(noun)*
Sentence: We believed, incorrectly, that the beautiful sunrise was a *propitious* sign.

PROPRIETY (pro-PRY-ih-tee) *noun* — **appropriateness; fitness**
Sentence: I wouldn't say the play was vulgar, but it did stretch the bounds of *propriety*.

PROSAIC (pro-ZAY-ik) *adj* — **common; dull; unimaginative**
Other form: Prosaically *(adv)*
Sentence: The teacher was tired of reading her students' *prosaic* essays.

PROSCRIBE (pro-SKRIBE) *verb* — **to forbid**
Other forms: Proscription *(noun);* proscriptive *(adj)*
Sentence: Scissors are *proscribed* items, and you cannot take them on an airplane.

PROTAGONIST (pro-TAG-uh-nist) *noun* — **the main character of a drama or story**
Sentence: By the end of the play, the *protagonist* must be changed in some way.

PROTEAN (PRO-tee-un) *adj* — **capable of assuming different forms or roles**
Other form: Protean *(noun)*
Sentence: We need a leader with a *protean* personality, someone who can adapt.

PROTOCOL (PRO-tuh-kawl) *noun* — **established set of rules and procedures**
Sentence: In the military, there is a *protocol* for just about every situation.

PROVIDENT (PROV-ih-dent) *adj* — **acting with forethought; prudent**
 Other forms: Providence *(noun);* providently *(adv)*
 Sentence: Her decision to get a degree was *provident*, and one she never regretted.

PROVINCIAL (pro-VINCH-shull) *adj* — **narrowly-focused; not worldly**
 Other forms: Provincialism *(noun);* provincially *(adv)*
 Sentence: Intimidated by her sophistication, he charmed her with his *provincialism*.

PROWESS (PROW-iss) *noun* — **extraordinary bravery or ability**
 Sentence: His *prowess* in the ring instilled fear in the other fighters.

PRUDENCE (PROO-dents) *noun* — **wisdom; cautiousness**
 Other forms: Prudent *(adj)*; prudently *(adv)*
 Sentence: Before you buy, it would be *prudent* to have the house inspected.

PRURIENT (PROOR-ee-int) *adj* — **insatiably curious, especially about sexual matters**
 Other forms: Prurience *(noun);* pruriently *(adv)*
 Sentence: Tabloids satisfy their readers' *prurient* need to know secrets about others.

PUGNACIOUS (pug-NAY-shuss) *adj* — **prone to fighting; belligerent**
 Other forms: Pugnaciously *(adv);* pugnacity *(noun)*
 Sentence: He was a *pugnacious* boy, and often came home with a black eye or two.

PUNCTILIOUS (punk-TIL-ee-us) *adj* — **attentive to detail, especially regarding rules of behavior**
 Other forms: Punctiliously *(adv);* punctiliousness *(noun)*
 Sentence: Worried about offending, we were *punctilious* about following their customs.

PUNDIT (PUN-dit) *noun* — **one who comes across as an expert; critic**
 Other form: Punditry *(noun)*
 Sentence: After her speech, the prime minister waited for the *pundits* to respond.

PUNGENT (PUN-jint) *adj* — **possessing a biting scent or flavor**
 Other forms: Pungency *(noun);* pungently *(adv)*
 Sentence: His *pungent* satire left no target unmarked.

PUNITIVE (PYOON-ih-tiv) *adj* — **serving to punish or penalize**
　　Other forms: Punitively *(adv)*; punitiveness *(noun)*
　　Sentence: The *punitive* damages awarded by the jury far exceeded the victim's losses.

PURLOIN (pur-LOYN) *verb* — **to wrongfully take; steal**
　　Sentence: The *purloined* jewels were never recovered.

PUSILLANIMOUS (pyoo-sill-AN-ih-mus) *adj* — **lacking strength or courage; cowardly**
　　Other forms: Pusillanimously *(adv)*; pusillanimousness *(noun)*
　　Sentence: Confronted directly, the bully turned out to be *pusillanimous* and frightened.

PYRE (PIRE) *noun* — **mound of wood to be torched, usually to burn a dead body**
　　Sentence: A large funeral *pyre* was prepared for the bodies of the fallen soldiers.

QUAFF (KWAFF) *verb* — **to drink freely and in abundance**
　　Other form: Quaffingly *(adv)*
　　Sentence: We watched in amazement as he *quaffed* one beer after another.

QUAINT (KWAYNT) *adj* — **artful or creative in an old-fashioned way**
　　Other forms: Quaintly *(adv)*; quaintness *(noun)*
　　Sentence: The *quaint* village made us feel as though we'd gone back in time.

QUALM (KWALM) *noun* — **a feeling of physical or emotional uneasiness**
　　Other forms: Qualmish *(adj)*; qualmishly *(adv)*
　　Sentence: He felt a *qualm* of regret for his action, even though he'd had no other choice.

QUIBBLE (KWIB-ul) *verb* — **to argue back and forth over a minor point**
　　Sentence: I agreed with his main idea, but we *quibbled* for days over the details.

QUIESCENCE (kwy-ESS-ents) *noun* — **stillness; inactivity**
　　Other forms: Quiescent *(adj)*; quiescently *(adv)*
　　Sentence: The *quiescence* on the lake's surface did not betray the turbulence below.

QUIESCENT (kwy-ESS-ent) *adj* — **idle; calm; latent**
Other forms: Quiescence *(noun);* quiescently *(adv)*
Sentence: The disease went into a *quiescent* period, and we thought he was cured.

QUIRK (KWIRK) *noun* — **a deviation from the norm; unusual trait**
Other forms: Quirkily *(adv)*; quirky *(adj)*
Sentence: In order to get along, roommates have to overlook each others' *quirks.*

QUIXOTIC (qwik-SOT-ik) *adj* — **romantically impractical; doomed to failure**
Other forms: Quixotical *(adj);* quixotically *(adv)*
Sentence: Many films are based on the hero's *quixotic* quest.

QUOTIDIAN (kwo-TID-ee-un) *adj* — **occurring every day; common**
Other form: Quotidian *(noun)*
Sentence: She dreamed of one day escaping her dull, *quotidian* routine.

RAFFISH (RAFF-ish) *adj* — **intentionally and dramatically unkempt; crude**
Other forms: Raffishly *(adv);* raffishness *(noun)*
Sentence: Pirates are often depicted as *raffishly* romantic characters.

RAMIFY (RAM-ih-fy) *verb* — **to split into branches; to spread by subdividing**
Other form: Ramification *(noun)*
Sentence: A teacher's wisdom can *ramify* and spread for generations.

RANCID (RAN-sid) *adj* — **decomposed, rotten**
Other forms: Rancidly *(adv);* rancidness *(noun)*
Sentence: Left in the warm room, the butter had turned *rancid.*

RANCOR (RANK-er) *noun* — **intense hatred**
Other forms: Rancorous *(adj);* rancorously *(adv)*
Sentence: The feuding families felt nothing but *rancor* for each other.

RANT (RANT) *noun* — **speech that is angry, irrational, or uncontrolled; tirade**
Other forms: Rant *(verb);* rantingly *(adv)*
Sentence: His unexpected *rant* troubled even his most loyal supporters.

RAPACIOUS (ruh-PAY-shuss) *adj* — **predatory; ravenous; voracious**
Other forms: Rapaciously *(adv);* rapaciousness *(noun)*
Sentence: The half-starved wolves launched a *rapacious* attack on the sheep.

RAUCOUS (RAW-kuss) *adj* — **loud; disorderly; boisterous**
Other forms: Raucously *(adv);* raucousness *(noun)*
Sentence: Our *raucous* behavior got us thrown out of the library.

RAZE (RAYZ) *verb* — **to destroy; to bring level to the ground**
Sentence: Several buildings were *razed* to make room for the new shopping center.

REACTIONARY (re-AK-shun-er-ee) *noun* — **person who wants things to return to the old ways; conservative**
Other forms: Reaction *(noun);* reactionary *(adj)*
Sentence: This modern artist surprised us with his *reactionary* political views.

RECALCITRANT (re-KAL-sih-trent) *adj* — **stubbornly resistant; defiant; unruly**
Other forms: Recalcitrance, recalcitrant, recalcitration *(nouns)*
Sentence: That breed of dog is naturally *recalcitrant* and can't be trained.

RECAPITULATE (re-kuh-PITCH-oo-layt) *verb* — **go over the main points; sum up**
Other forms: Recapitulation *(noun);* recapitulative *(adj)*
Sentence: His job as secretary was to *recapitulate* what was said at the meetings.

RECIDIVISM (re-SID-ih-viz-um) *noun* — **a return to old behaviors; tendency to relapse**
Other forms: Recidivate *(verb);* recidivist *(noun);* recidivous *(adj)*
Sentence: The rate of *recidivism* among alcoholics is very high.

RECIPROCAL (re-SIP-ruh-kul) *adj* — **common; mutual**
Other forms: Reciprocally *(adv);* reciprocate *(verb);* reciprocation *(noun)*
Sentence: Loyalty between the brothers was *reciprocal*: they always defended each other.

RECIPROCATE (re-SIP-ro-kayt) *verb* — **to respond in an equal or similar manner**
Other forms: Reciprocal *(adj);* reciprocally *(adv);* reciprocation *(noun)*
Sentence: She had sent me a gift, so I felt compelled to *reciprocate*.

RECIPROCITY (ress-ih-PROSS-ih-tee) *noun* — **mutual exchange of courtesies or concessions between two individuals or groups**
Other forms: Reciprocal *(adj)*; reciprocally *(adv)*; reciprocation *(noun)*
Sentence: There was an unspoken *reciprocity* of aid between the two ravaged nations.

RECONCILE (REK-un-sile) *verb* — **to restore to harmony; to settle or accept**
Other forms: Reconciliation *(noun)*; reconciliatory *(adj)*
Sentence: He had finally *reconciled* himself to the idea that she was never coming back.

RECTIFY (REK-tih-fy) *verb* — **to make right; to correct**
Other forms: Rectifiable *(adj)*; rectifiably *(adv)*; rectification *(noun)*
Sentence: The boys tried to *rectify* their mistake my returning what they had stolen.

RECTITUDE (REK-tih-tood) *noun* — **rightness; straightness; correctness**
Other forms: Rectitudinous *(adj)*; rectitudinously *(adv)*
Sentence: Her sense of *rectitude* helped her continue, even when others doubted.

REDOUBTABLE (re-DOWT-uh-bull) *adj* — **inspiring awe or reverence**
Other form: Redoubtably *(adv)*
Sentence: Her *redoubtable* skills as a speaker made her a formidable trial attorney.

REDRESS (REE-dress) *noun* — **compensation for an offense or loss; reparation**
Other form: Redress *(verb)*
Sentence: Their land had been taken, and now they sought *redress* from the governor.

REFRACT (re-FRAKT) *verb* — **to bend or distort**
Other forms: Refraction *(noun)*; refractive *(adj)*; refractively *(adv)*
Sentence: Light slows down when passing through glass, so it is *refracted*.

REFRACTORY (re-FRAK-ter-ee) *adj* — **resistant; unruly; stubborn**
Other forms: Refractorily *(adv)*
Sentence: I was the good child; my *refractory* twin wouldn't listen to anyone.

REFUTE (re-FYOOT) *verb* — **to disprove**
Other forms: Refutable *(adj)*; refutably *(adv)*; refutation *(noun)*
Sentence: She was able to *refute* the theory with very ordinary evidence.

REGALE (re-GAYL) *verb* — **to lavish with treats or entertainment; to please**
    Other form: Regalement *(noun)*
    Sentence: After his trip, he *regaled* us with stories of exotic lands.

REITERATE (re-IT-er-ayt) *verb* — **to repeat a statement or action over and over**
    Other forms: Reiteration *(noun)*; reiterative *(adj)*; reiteratively *(adv)*
    Sentence: We *reiterated* the instructions to make sure everyone understood.

RELAPSE (re-LAPS) *verb* — **to slip back to a former condition**
    Other form: Relapse *(noun)*
    Sentence: Many people who climb out of debt eventually *relapse* into their old ways.

RELINQUISH (re-LINK-wish) *verb* — **to give up; surrender; yield**
    Other form: Relinquishment *(noun)*
    Sentence: Land taken by force is rarely *relinquished* voluntarily.

RELISH (REL-ish) *verb* — **to take great pleasure from**
    Other forms: Relish *(noun)*; relishable *(adj)*
    Sentence: We *relished* the idea of seeing our old friends again.

REMINISCENT (reh-min-ISS-ent) *adj* — **triggering memories or describing past experiences**
    Other forms: Reminisce *(verb)*; reminiscence *(noun)*
    Sentence: The party was *reminiscent* of celebrations from my childhood.

REMISS (re-MISS) *adj* — **careless; negligent**
    Sentence: A policeman who is *remiss* in his duties can cause injury to others.

REMONSTRATE (REM-un-strayt) *verb* — **to plead against; to object; to protest**
    Other forms: Remonstrance, remonstration *(nouns)*; remonstrative *(adj)*
    Sentence: We tried to *remonstrate* the decision, but the judge dismissed us.

RENAISSANCE (REN-uh-sants) *noun* — **a period of revival or rebirth**
    Other form: Renaissance *(adj)*
    Sentence: After years of *inactivity*, that style is enjoying a renaissance.

RENDER (REN-der) *verb* — **hand over; transmit; provide**
Sentence: They travel the world, *rendering* whatever help they can to the needy.

RENOVATE (REN-oh-vayt) *verb* — **to make new again; refurbish**
Other form: Renovation *(noun)*
Sentence: My plans to *renovate* the old house were blocked by the historical society.

RENUNCIATION (re-nun-see-AY-shun) *noun* — **to resign, abandon, or sacrifice**
Other form: Renounce *(verb)*
Sentence: His *renunciation* of the office was a signal that he had his sights on a new goal.

REPARATION (rep-er-AY-shun) *noun* — **an act intended to make amends**
Other forms: Repair *(verb);* reparative *(adj)*
Sentence: The company built a new hospital as *reparation* for the ecological disaster.

REPLENISH (re-PLEN-ish) *verb* — **to refill or resupply**
Other form: Replenishment *(noun)*
Sentence: The waiter at the fancy restaurant *replenished* my water every time I took a sip.

REPLETE (re-PLEET) *adj* — **filled to capacity; complete**
Other forms: Replete *(verb);* repletion *(noun);* repletive *(adj)*
Sentence: This history book is *replete* with photographs, drawings, and maps.

REPOSE (re-POZE) *noun* — **a state of rest; tranquility**
Other forms: Repose *(verb);* reposeful *(adj);* reposefully *(adv)*
Sentence: One statue depicted a child in *repose*, and his watchful mother.

REPREHENSIBLE (rep-ree-HEN-sih-bull) *adj* — **deserving of criticism; blamable**
Other form: Reprehensibly *(adv)*
Sentence: The bride was embarrassed by her sister's *reprehensible* behavior.

REPRIEVE (re-PREEV) *noun* — **a postponement of something unpleasant**
Other form: Reprieve *(verb)*
Sentence: His *reprieve* was short-lived; he was punished the next day.

REPROACH (re-PROACH) *noun* — **expression of disapproval; or a state of disgrace**
    Other forms: Reproach *(verb)*; reproachable *(adv)*; reproachful *(adj)*
    Sentence: No longer able to keep quiet, she hurled one *reproach* after another at him.

REPROBATE (REP-ro-bayt) *noun* — **one who is corrupt; scoundrel**
    Other forms: Reprobate *(adj)*; reprobate *(verb)*; reprobation *(noun)*
    Sentence: Eventually, even his family considered him a hopeless *reprobate*.

REPULSE (re-PULSE) *verb* — **to force back; reject; repel**
    Other forms: Repulse *(noun)*; repulsion *(noun)*
    Sentence: From the hilltop castle, it was easy to *repulse* the invading army.

REQUISITE (REK-wiz-it) *adj* — **necessary; essential; unavoidable**
    Other forms: Requisite, requisition *(nouns)*
    Sentence: A curious mind is *requisite* for scientific inquiry.

REQUITE (re-KWITE) *verb* — **to pay back; reciprocate**
    Other forms: Requital *(noun)*; requited *(adj)*
    Sentence: His faith in the people was later *requited* by their total support for him.

RESCIND (re-SIND) *verb* — **to remove; cancel; annul; revoke**
    Other forms: Rescindable *(adj)*; rescission *(noun)*
    Sentence: After much public protest, the law was *rescinded*.

RESILIENCE (re-ZIL-yents) *noun* — **the ability to rebound from adversity; elasticity**
    Other forms: Resilient *(adj)*; resiliently *(adv)*
    Sentence: Space suits must provide both *resilience* and comfort.

RESOLUTE (REZ-uh-loot) *adj* — **unwavering; determined**
    Other forms: Resolutely *(adv)*; resolution *(noun)*; resolve *(verb)*
    Sentence: She was *resolute* in her decision, and she never gave up.

RESONANCE (REZ-uh-nents) *noun* — **enrichment; reinforcement; harmony**
    Other forms: Resonant *(adj)*; resonantly *(adv)*; resonate *(verb)*
    Sentence: Individually pleasant, their two voices produced a beautiful *resonance*.

RESPITE (RESS-pit) *noun* — **postponement; reprieve; delay**
Other form: Respite *(verb)*
Sentence: The holy days provided a *respite* for the soldiers on both sides.

RESPLENDENT (re-SPLEN-dent) *adj* — **shining brilliantly**
Other forms: Resplendence *(noun);* resplendently *(adv)*
Sentence: In her dream, an angel appeared as a *resplendent* being.

RESTITUTION (ress-tih-TOO-shun) *noun* — **repayment; restoration**
Other form: Restitute *(verb)*
Sentence: The convicted man was ordered to pay *restitution* to his victim's family.

RESTIVE (RESS-tiv) *adj* — **ill at ease; fidgety**
Other forms: Restively *(adv);* restiveness *(noun)*
Sentence: As the plane sat idle, the passengers grew *restive* and nervous.

RETRACT (re-TRAKT) *verb* — **to pull back, either physically or verbally; withdraw**
Other forms: Retractable *(adj)*; retraction *(noun)*
Sentence: Under pressure, the witness *retracted* her statement from the previous day.

RETROSPECTIVE (reh-tro-SPEK-tiv) *adj* — **looking back; remembering**
Other forms: Retrospection *(noun)*; retrospective *(noun)*; retrospectively *(adv)*
Sentence: The film was a *retrospective* look at explorers of the 18th century.

REVERENT (REV-rent) *adj* — **holding in the highest respect**
Other forms: Revere *(verb);* reverence *(noun);* reverential *(adj);* reverently *(adv)*
Sentence: It's important to be *reverent* when in another person's place of worship.

REVOKE (re-VOKE) *verb* — **cancel; repeal; annul**
Other forms: Revocation *(noun)*; revocative *(adj)*
Sentence: If you're caught driving while intoxicated, the court can *revoke* your license.

RIBALD (RY-bald) *adj* — **coarse; offensive; indecent**
Other forms: Ribaldly *(adv);* ribaldry *(noun)*
Sentence: His *ribald* jokes were unwelcome at our solemn gathering.

RIFE (RIFE) *adj* — **filled; overflowing**
    Other form: Rifeness *(noun)*
    Sentence: The town was *rife* with rumors about the new family.

RIGOROUS (RIG-er-uss) *adj* — **requiring exertion; strict; exacting**
    Other forms: Rigor *(noun);* rigorously *(adv)*
    Sentence: The training was *rigorous*, and many people dropped out.

ROBUST (ro-BUST) *adj* — **exhibiting great strength, energy, or stamina**
    Other forms: Robustly *(adv);* robustness *(noun)*
    Sentence: He was surprisingly *robust* for a man of that age.

RUFFIAN (RUFF-ee-in) *noun* — **a coarse, brutish man; troublemaker; bully**
    Other forms: Ruffian *(adj);* ruffianism *(noun)*
    Sentence: In one year, he transformed from *ruffian* to businessman.

RUMINATE (ROO-min-ayt) *verb* — **to chew on; to think about over and over**
    Other form: Rumination *(noun);* ruminative *(adj);* ruminatively *(adv)*
    Sentence: She was left alone to *ruminate* about her actions.

RUSE (ROOZ) *noun* — **trick; deception**
    Sentence: It was amazing how many people had fallen for the *ruse*, and lost money.

RUSTIC (RUSS-tik) *adj* — **related to rural areas; rough; not polished or modern**
    Sentence: It was just what we wanted: a *rustic* cabin, with no modern conveniences.

SACRILEGE (SAK-ruh-lij) *noun* — **an act of violating or desecrating something holy**
    Other forms: Sacrilegious *(adj);* sacrilegiously *(adv)*
    Sentence: To the church officials, the theft was more than a crime; it was a *sacrilege*.

SACROSANCT (SAK-ro-sankt) *adj* — **having a high degree of holiness; most sacred**
    Other form: Sacrosanctity *(noun)*
    Sentence: The most orthodox believe that fasting is *sacrosanct*.

SAGACITY (suh-GAS-ih-tee) *noun* — **a piercing ability to comprehend**
Other forms: Sagacious (*adj*); sagaciously *(adv)*
Sentence: In China, Confucius is considered a model of *sagacity*.

SALACIOUS (suh-LAY-shuss) *adj* — **lustful; obscene**
Other forms: Salaciously *(adv);* salaciousness *(noun)*
Sentence: She was shocked by the *salacious* material she found in her son's room.

SALIENT (SAIL-yent) *adj* — **prominent; noticeable**
Other forms: Saliency *(noun);* saliently *(adv)*
Sentence: There were a few *salient* passages in an otherwise empty narrative.

SALUTATION (sal-yoo-TAY-shun) *noun* — **a word or gesture of tribute; greeting**
Other forms: Salutatorily *(adv)*; salutatory *(adj)*
Sentence: The host offered *salutations* to everyone in attendance.

SANCTIMONIOUS (sank-tih-MONE-ee-us) *adj* — **insincerely pious or religious**
Other forms: Sanctimoniously *(adv);* sanctimony *(noun)*
Sentence: Despite his *sanctimonious* statements, we knew his intentions were bad.

SAPIENT (SAY-pee-int) *adj* — **possessing wisdom; sagacious**
Other forms: Sapience *(noun);* sapiently *(adv)*
Sentence: Right from birth, the tribe considered him to be a *sapient* spirit.

SARCOPHAGUS (sar-KOFF-ih-gus) *noun* — **stone coffin, often carved**
Sentence: We found his *sarcophagus* in one of the dark recesses of the cathedral.

SATIATE (SAY-shee-ayt) *verb* — **to fill or satisfy**
Other form: Satiate (*adj*); satiety *(noun)*
Sentence: The feast left us so *satiated*, it was hard to imagine ever eating again.

SATURNINE (SAT-er-nine) *adj* — **morose; sullen; melancholy**
Other form: Saturninity *(noun)*
Sentence: I've been to funerals that weren't as *saturnine* as that party.

SAVANT (suh-VANT) *noun* — **person with a deep knowledge in a specific field**
Sentence: She is a musical *savant*, and has been writing symphonies since she was three.

SCABBARD (SKAB-erd) *noun* — **a leather or metal sheath for safely carrying a blade**
Sentence: After slaying the dragon, he returned his sword to its *scabbard*.

SCURRILOUS (SKUR-ih-luss) *adj* — **marked by base language; coarse; obscene**
Other forms: Scurrilously *(adv)*; scurrilousness *(noun)*
Sentence: That newspaper is filled with *scurrilous* lies and fabrications.

SEDATE (suh-DAYT) *adj* — **calm; relaxed; peaceful**
Other forms: Sedate *(verb)*; sedately *(adv)*; sedation, sedative *(nouns)*; sedative *(adj)*
Sentence: The sailboat seemed to float *sedately* over the waves.

SEDENTARY (SED-en-terr-ee) *adj* — **remaining in one place; stationary; seated**
Other forms: Sedentarily *(adv)*; sedentariness *(noun)*
Sentence: You have an even greater need for exercise, given your *sedentary* lifestyle.

SEDULOUS (SEJ-oo-luss) *adj* — **industrious; diligent**
Other forms: Sedulously *(adv)*; sedulousness *(noun)*
Sentence: His *sedulous* approach to his work is apparent in the wonderful results.

SEMINAL (SEM-in-ul) *adj* — **leading to subsequent results; original**
Other forms: Seminality *(noun)*; seminally *(adv)*
Sentence: Greek mythology played a *seminal* role in the development of later stories.

SENSUOUS (SEN-shoo-us) *adj* — **having to do with the senses; pleasurable**
Other forms: Sensuality *(noun)*; sensuously *(adv)*
Sentence: A trip through a tropical rain forest must be a *sensuous* experience.

SENTINEL (SEN-tih-nel) *noun* — **one who keeps watch; guard**
Sentence: There was a *sentinel* posted at every gate, so escape was not likely.

SEQUENCE (SEE-kwents) *noun* — **an arrangement of elements; progression**
 Other forms: Sequential *(adj)*; sequentially *(adv)*
 Sentence: Events in a dream sometimes seem out of *sequence*.

SEQUESTER (seh-KWES-ter) *verb* — **to remove or separate for a purpose; segregate**
 Other forms: Sequestered *(adj)*; sequestration *(noun)*
 Sentence: The men and women were *sequestered* in separate rooms.

SERENDIPITY (serr-en-DIP-ih-tee) *noun* — **happy coincidence; unexpected result**
 Other forms: Serendipitous *(adj)*; serendipitously *(adv)*
 Sentence: Our friends met at our wedding, and it was *serendipity*: now they're married!

SERENE (suh-REEN) *adj* — **calm; quiet; soothingly peaceful**
 Other forms: Serenely *(adv)*; serenity *(noun)*
 Sentence: When I need to relax, I imagine a *serene* beach with gentle waves.

SERRATED (suh-RAY-tid) *adj* — **marked by peaks and ridges; saw-toothed**
 Other form: Serrate *(verb)*; serration *(noun)*
 Sentence: It's easier to cut bread with a *serrated* knife.

SEVERANCE (SEV-er-ents) *noun* — **separation; disconnection**
 Other forms: Sever *(verb)*; severed *(adj)*
 Sentence: There was a *severance* among the units, as though they were distinct companies.

SINISTER (SIN-iss-ter) *adj* — **evil; wicked**
 Other form: Sinisterly *(adv)*
 Sentence: They discovered his *sinister* plan just in time: people could have been killed.

SINUOUS (SIN-yoo-uss) *adj* — **bending in and out; wavy; serpentine**
 Other forms: Sinuously *(adv)*; sinuosity, sinuousness *(nouns)*
 Sentence: The river followed a *sinuous* path, winding around hills and down to the lake.

SKIFF (SKIFF) *noun* — **a small, light boat**
 Sentence: She rowed the *skiff* silently through the still water.

SLUGGARD (SLUG-erd) *noun* — **one who lacks motivation; lazy person**
   Other forms: Sluggard (*adj*); sluggardly *(adv)*; sluggardness *(noun)*
   Sentence: We all had to do extra work to make up for the *sluggard* down the hall.

SODDEN (SOD-en) *adj* — **soaked with a liquid, especially alcohol**
   Other forms: Soddenly *(adv)*; soddenness *(noun)*
   Sentence: After eight hours at the bar, he was a *sodden*, sweating mess.

SOLACE (SOLL-iss) *noun* — **relief from grief; consolation**
   Other form: Solaceful (*adj*)
   Sentence: Even in our devastation, we could find *solace* in memories.

SOLICITOUS (suh-LISS-ih-tuss) *adj* — **anxiously attentive; apprehensive**
   Other forms: Solicitously *(adv)*; solicitude *(noun)*
   Sentence: New parents are often *solicitous* about their baby's health.

SOLUBLE (SOL-yoo-bull) *adj* — **capable of being dissolved; also, solvable**
   Other forms: Solubility *(noun)*; solubly *(adv)*
   Sentence: A certain amount of salt is *soluble* in a certain amount of water.

SOLVENT (SOL-vent) *adj* — **able to pay one's debts; also, something that can cause another substance to dissolve**
   Other form: Solvency (*noun*)
   Sentence: The bank determined that the business was *solvent*, and approved the loan.

SOMNOLENT (SOM-nuh-lent) *adj* — **tending to cause drowsiness; sleepy**
   Other forms: Somnolence *(noun)*; somnolently *(adv)*
   Sentence: The philosophy professor had a *somnolent* effect on many of his students.

SOPHISTRY (SO-fiss-tree) *noun* — **ideas that seem rational and true, but are not**
   Other form: Sophist (*noun*)
   Sentence: A dictator on the rise will often indulge in *sophistry* and propaganda.

SOPHOMORIC (soff-uh-MOR-ik) *adj* — **unaware of limitations; inexperienced**
   Sentence: My arguments were silly and *sophomoric*, but they made sense to me.

SOPORIFIC (sop-er-IF-ik) *adj* — **in a stupor; drowsy**
 Other forms: Sopor (*noun*); soporiferous (*adj*); soporiferously *(adv)*
 Sentence: After fourteen hours of driving, we were all *soporific* zombies.

SORDID (SOR-did) *adj* — **filthy; foul; corrupt; vile**
 Other forms: Sordidly *(adv);* sordidness (*noun*)
 Sentence: It was an evil, *sordid* plot, and we wanted nothing to do with it.

SPLENETIC (spleh-NET-ik) *adj* — **bad-tempered; spiteful; irritable**
 Other form: Splenetically (*adv*)
 Sentence: My uncle was unpredictable: one minute *splenetic*, the next quite pleasant.

SPONTANEOUS (spon-TAY-nee-us) *adj* — **acting without plan or forethought; sudden**
 Other forms: Spontaneity *(noun);* spontaneously *(adv)*
 Sentence: Our decision to move to New Zealand was *spontaneous*, and surprised even us.

SPURN (SPURN) *verb* — **to speak out against in harsh terms; reject; scorn**
 Other form: Spurned *(adj)*
 Sentence: Gandhi *spurned* the use of violence, choosing peaceful protest instead.

SQUALID (SKWAH-lid) *adj* — **filthy; shabby; unwholesome; sordid**
 Other forms: Squalor (*noun*); squalidly *(adv)*
 Sentence: I knew they lived in poverty, but was still shocked by the *squalid* conditions.

STAGNATE (STAG-nayt) *verb* — **to remain motionless; fail to progress**
 Other forms: Stagnant (*adj*); stagnantly (*adv*); stagnation (*noun*)
 Sentence: A little success causes some people to *stagnate*, and they stop developing.

STAID (STAYD) *adj* — **serious; grave; unenthusiastic**
 Other forms: Staidly (*adv*); staidness (*noun*)
 Sentence: His *staid* demeanor was not what you'd expect of a professional clown.

STANCH (STANCH) *verb* — **to stop the flow of something**
 Other form: Stanch (*noun*)
 Sentence: By building a factory, they could *stanch* the flow of dollars to other nations.

STIGMA (STIG-muh) *noun* — **mark of shame; the result of a disgraceful trait or action**
    Other form: Stigmatize *(verb)*
    Sentence: He could never escape the *stigma* of his father's imprisonment.

STIPEND (STY-pend) *noun* — **small salary or allowance paid for services**
    Other form: Stipendiary *(adj)*
    Sentence: The *stipend* I received barely paid for the gasoline I used driving to work.

STOLID (STAHL-id) *adj* — **not easily aroused; unexcitable**
    Other forms: Stolidity *(noun)*; stolidly *(adv)*
    Sentence: He was an old and *stolid* dog, not interested in playing with the children.

STRIDENT (STRY-dent) *adj* — **harsh-sounding; loudly overbearing**
    Other forms: Stridence *(noun)*; stridently *(adv)*
    Sentence: Your *strident* tone is making everyone tense and tired.

STRINGENT (STRIN-jent) *adj* — **strict; rigid; severe**
    Other forms: Stringency *(noun)*; stringently *(adv)*
    Sentence: The school's *stringent* rules were meant to promote learning and discipline.

STUPEFY (STOO-ph-fy) *verb* — **to stun; to put into a trance or daze**
    Other forms: Stupefaction *(noun)*; stupefying *(adj)*; stupefyingly *(adv)*
    Sentence: After months of digging, we were *stupefied* by what we finally found.

SUBMISSIVE (sub-MISS-iv) *adj* — **tame; obedient; willing to yield**
    Other forms: Submissively *(adv)*; submissiveness *(noun)*; submit *(verb)*
    Sentence: Within two days, the hostage became *submissive* and did whatever he was told.

SUBPOENA (suh-PEE-nuh) *verb* — **an official order to attend a hearing**
    Other form: Subpoena *(noun)*
    Sentence: I was warned that the court would *subpoena* me if I didn't come voluntarily.

SUBSTANTIATE (sub-STAN-chee-ayt) *verb* — **to provide proof of an assertion; confirm**
    Other forms: Substantiation *(noun)*; substantiative *(adj)*
    Sentence: She could not *substantiate* her claims and the case was dropped.

SUBTERFUGE (SUB-ter-fyooj) *noun* — **a deceptive device or plan; trickery**
Sentence: Your *subterfuge* was totally unnecessary: we would have given you the money.

SUBVERSIVE (sub-VER-siv) *adj* — **tending to destroy or overthrow, often from within**
Other forms: Subversion *(noun)*; subversively *(adv)*; subvert *(verb)*
Sentence: The group's *subversive* activity almost brought down the entire government.

SUNDRY (SUN-dree) *adj* — **assorted; several**
Other forms: Sundry *(adv)*
Sentence: He carried *sundry* family photos in his wallet.

SUPERCILIOUS (soo-per-SILL-ee-us) *adj* — **scornful; sneering; disdainful**
Other forms: Superciliously *(adv)*; superciliousness *(noun)*
Sentence: Her *supercilious* attitude in the office alienated her employees.

SUPERFICIAL (soo-per-FISH-ul) *adj* — **on the surface; not deep or sincere**
Other forms: Superficiality *(noun)*; superficially *(adv)*
Sentence: His involvement was *superficial*, and deep down he didn't really care.

SUPERSEDE (soo-per-SEED) *verb* — **to overthrow or make obsolete; replace**
Other forms: Supersession *(noun)*; supersessive *(adj)*
Sentence: In some situations, your love of another person *supersedes* your own interests.

SUPINE (SOO-pine) *adj* — **lying face up; on the back**
Other forms: Supinate *(verb)*; supination *(noun)*; supinely *(adv)*
Sentence: He was *supine* on the grass, fast asleep in the field.

SUPPLANT (suh-PLANT) *verb* — **to overthrow; supersede; replace**
Other form: Supplantation *(noun)*
Sentence: Attempts to *supplant* the team's coaching staff was met with fan protests.

SUPPLE (SUP-ul) *adj* — **bendable; pliable; adaptable**
Other form: Suppleness *(noun)*
Sentence: His *supple* mind was able to absorb the strange language in a few weeks.

SUPPLICATE (SUP-lih-kayt) *verb* — **to humble oneself in order to plead; beg**
  Other forms: Supplicatingly *(adv)*; supplication *(noun)*
  Sentence: Fearing they would be killed, the hostages *supplicated* to the kidnappers.

SUPPRESS (suh-PRESS) *verb* — **to stifle or subdue; to prevent from escaping**
  Other forms: Suppression *(noun)*; suppressive *(adj)*
  Sentence: Her family somehow managed to *suppress* the news about tragedy.

SURFEIT (SUR-fet) *noun* — **an overabundance of something; excess**
  Other form: Surfeit *(verb)*
  Sentence: There was such a *surfeit* of books, more than we could ever read.

SURMISE (sur-MYZE) *verb* — **to suppose or guess based on little evidence; conjecture**
  Other forms: Surmisable *(adj)*; surmise *(noun)*
  Sentence: We *surmise* that the burglar came in through a window, but we're not sure.

SURROGATE (SUR-uh-gut) *adj* — **standing in place of someone else; substituting**
  Other forms: Surrogacy, surrogate *(nouns)*
  Sentence: We asked him to be our *surrogate* at the meeting, because we could not attend.

SUSCEPTIBILITY (suh-sep-tuh-BILL-ih-tee) *noun* — **the ability to be affected**
  Other forms: Susceptible *(adj)*
  Sentence: Your *susceptibility* to the flu makes you a poor candidate for space flight.

SYBARITE (SIB-uh-ryte) *noun* — **person devoted to pleasure and luxury**
  Other form: Sybaritic *(adj)*
  Sentence: To prepare for her new life as a *sybarite*, she moved into a casino hotel.

SYNOPSIS (sin-OP-siss) *noun* — **a brief summary giving an overview of the whole**
  Other forms: Synopsize *(verb)*; synoptic *(adj)*
  Sentence: Your *synopsis* was so good, I didn't have to read the book.

TACIT (TASS-it) *adj* — **with few words; unspoken; understood**
  Other forms: Tacitly *(adv)*; tacitness *(noun)*; taciturn *(adj)*
    Sentence: They had a *tacit* agreement that neither would go after the other's customers.

TANGENTIAL (tan-JEN-shull) *adj* — **deviating from the intended subject**
Other forms: Tangent *(noun);* tangentially *(adv)*
Sentence: I'm afraid my comments are *tangential* and won't add to the discussion.

TANGIBLE (TAN-jih-bull) *adj* — **able to be seen, touched, or perceived**
Other forms: Tangibility *(noun)*; tangibly *(adv)*
Sentence: He found algebra too abstract, preferring the *tangible* nature of geometry.

TAUT (TAWT) *adj* — **tightly wound or drawn; containing no extra parts; spare**
Other forms: Tautly *(adv)*; tautness *(noun)*
Sentence: The story was *taut*: no superfluous scenes or characters, every element essential.

TAUTOLOGY (taw-TOL-ih-jee) *noun* — **a repetitive statement; redundancy**
Other forms: Tautological *(adj)*; tautologically *(adv)*; tautologism *(noun)*
Sentence: Her speech could have been much shorter were it not for all the *tautologies*.

TAWDRY (TAW-jree) *adj* — **cheaply showy or gaudy; low class**
Other forms: Tawdrily *(adv)*; tawdriness *(noun)*
Sentence: She claimed to prefer the finer things, but her appearance was *tawdry*.

TEMERITY (teh-MER-ih-tee) *noun* — **courage bordering on the foolhardy; brashness**
Other forms: Temerarious *(adj)*; temerariously *(adv)*
Sentence: That you had the *temerity* to interrupt us is a reflection of your foolishness.

TEMPERANCE (TEM-per-ents) *noun* — **moderation; self-control; restraint**
Sentence: As you get older and settle down, a certain degree of *temperance* takes over.

TENABLE (TEN-uh-bull) *adj* — **capable of being defended; reasonable**
Other forms: Tenableness *(noun)*; tenably *(adv)*
Sentence: Your position is not *tenable*, and the obvious choice is to abandon it.

TOME (TOME) *noun* — **a thick book; a comprehensive volume**
Sentence: He tends to be wordy: his shortest *tome* is a thousand pages.

TORRID (TORR-id) *adj* — **hot; feverish; passionate**
Other form: Torridness *(noun);* torridly *(adv)*
Sentence: The *torrid* temperature drained us and we had no energy to do anything.

TORTUOUS (TOR-choo-uss) *adj* — **twisting; winding; difficult to navigate**
Other form: Tortuously *(adv);* tortuousness *(noun)*
Sentence: A large car would not handle well on those *tortuous* roads.

TRACTABLE (TRAK-tuh-bull) *adj* — **controllable; yielding; obedient**
Other forms: Tractability *(noun);* tractably *(adv)*
Sentence: He was a *tractable* witness and each side got him to support their case.

TRANQUIL (TRAN-kwil) *adj* — **free from agitation; peaceful; serene**
Other forms: Tranquility *(noun);* tranquilize *(verb);* tranquilly *(adv)*
Sentence: After five turbulent months, she finally felt *tranquil* again.

TRANSGRESS (trans-GRESS) *verb* — **to violate a rule or boundary; to "cross the line"**
Other forms: Transgression *(noun)*; transgressive *(adj)*
Sentence: You've inadvertently *transgressed* into an illegal area.

TRANSIENT (TRAN-ze-ent) *adj* — **short-lived; temporary; ephemeral**
Other forms: Transience *(noun);* transiently *(adv)*
Sentence: Those are *transient* circumstances, and when you return they will be gone.

TRANSITORY (TRAN-zih-tor-ee) *adj* — **appearing and disappearing quickly**
Other forms: Transitorily *(adv);* transitoriness *(noun)*
Sentence: Dreams are often *transitory*, lasting just a few seconds and then forgotten.

TRANSMUTE (trans-MYOOT) *verb* — **to change in form or nature; convert**
Other forms: Transmutable *(adj)*; transmutation *(noun)*
Sentence: For centuries, people tried to *transmute* lead into gold.

TRAVESTY (TRAV-es-tee) *noun* — **a bad imitation; gross deficiency**
Sentence: What they intended to be *Hamlet* was nothing more than a *travesty*.

TREMULOUS (TREM-yoo-luss) *adj* — **shaking; quivering**
    Other forms: Tremulously (*adv*); tremulousness *(noun)*
    Sentence: The police knew from her meek and *tremulous* replies that she was scared.

TRENCHANT (TREN-chent) *adj* — **extremely effective; penetrating; incisive**
    Other forms: Trenchancy *(noun);* trenchantly *(adv)*
    Sentence: She won the debate with *trenchant*, concise, and consistent arguments.

TRUNCATE (TRUN-kayt) *verb* — **to shorten; abbreviate; abridge**
    Other forms: Truncated (*adj*); truncation (*noun*)
    Sentence: The tennis match ran long, so the network *truncated* the movie that followed.

TURBID (TUR-bid) *adj* — **cloudy; muddy; unclear**
    Other forms: Turbidity (*noun*); turbidly (*adv*)
    Sentence: Racism is usually characterized by a set of *turbid* and contradictory beliefs.

TURGID (TUR-jid) *adj* — **swollen; bloated; inflated**
    Other forms: Turgidity *(noun);* turgidly *(adv)*
    Sentence: Her face was *turgid*, an allergic reaction to the drug.

TURPITUDE (TURP-ih-tood) *noun* — **baseness; vileness; depravity**
    Sentence: He found every kind of moral *turpitude* within a week of moving to the city.

ULTERIOR (ul-TEER-ee-er) *adj* — **beyond the obvious; hidden; latent**
    Other form: Ulteriorly (*adv*)
    Sentence: We didn't learn of her *ulterior* motives until it was too late.

UMBRAGE (UM-brij) *noun* — **resentment; displeasure**
    Other forms: Umbrageous (*adj*); umbrageously (*adv*)
    Sentence: I have to take *umbrage* at the rude tone in your voice.

UNBRIDLED (un-BRYD-uld) *adj* — **enthusiastic; free; unrestrained**
    Other form: Unbridle (*verb*)
    Sentence: Her face shone with *unbridled* love when she saw her son again.

UNCONSCIONABLE (un-KAHN-shun-uh-bull) *adj* — **shocking; unforgivable**
Other forms: Unconscionably *(adv)*
Sentence: Their actions were *unconscionable*, and ultimately led to war.

UNCTUOUS (UNK-shoo-uss) *adj* — **oily; greasy; falsely earnest**
Other forms: Unctuously *(adv)*; unctuousness *(noun)*
Sentence: His slick and *unctuous* manner told us all to beware.

UNTOWARD (un-TOW-erd) *adj* — **difficult to manage; adverse; improper**
Other forms: Untowardly *(adv)*; untowardness *(noun)*
Sentence: We faced a long series of *untoward* events, and finally had to give up.

UNWITTING (un-WIT-ing) *adj* — **unaware; oblivious; accidental**
Other form: Unwittingly *(adv)*
Sentence: I had *unwittingly* ruined the surprise, much to everyone's disappointment.

URBANE (ur-BANE) *adj* — **worldly; polished; suave**
Other forms: Urbanely *(adv);* urbanity *(noun)*
Sentence: I felt unsophisticated and felt out of place among those *urbane* people.

UTILITARIAN (yoo-till-ih-TARE-ee-un) *adj* — **practical; functional**
Other form: Utilitarianism *(noun)*
Sentence: She abandoned her fancy wardrobe for more *utilitarian* clothes.

VALOROUS (VAL-er-uss) *adj* — **courageous**
Other forms: Valor *(noun);* valorously *(adv)*
Sentence: He received three medals for *valorous* action in combat.

VARIEGATE (VAR-ee-uh-gayt) *verb* — **to add variety; diversify**
Other forms: Variegated *(adj)*; variegation *(noun)*
Sentence: We sprinkled in different kinds of seeds, hoping to *variegate* the garden.

VEHEMENT (VEE-uh-ment) *adj* — **with great force or passion; ardent**
Other forms: Vehemence *(noun)*; vehemently *(adv)*
Sentence: He was so *vehement* about his position, that we all agreed to do it his way.

VENAL (VEE-nul) *adj* — **capable of being bought; open to corruption**
Other forms: Venality (*noun*); venally (*adv*)
Sentence: The company had a *venal* arrangement with the dishonest mayor.

VENEER (vuh-NEER) *noun* — **thin outer surface used for show; superficial appearance**
Other form: Veneer (*verb*)
Sentence: His *veneer* of sincerity masks a deceitful obsession.

VENERATE (VEN-er-ayt) *verb* — **to revere; honor**
Other form: Veneration *(noun)*
Sentence: In some cultures, children still *venerate* parents and grandparents.

VENIAL (VEE-nee-ul) *adj* — **relatively insignificant; forgivable; excusable**
Other form: Venially (*adv*)
Sentence: Other than a few *venial* offenses, your record is perfect.

VERACIOUS (ver-AY-shuss) *adj* — **truthful; accurate**
Other form: Veraciously (*adv*); veracity *(noun)*
Sentence: His testimony was deemed to be *veracious* and based entirely on the facts.

VERDANT (VER-dant) *adj* — **green with vegetation; also, inexperienced**
Other form: Verdantly *(adv)*
Sentence: The *verdant* river valley contrasted sharply with the surrounding desert.

VERISIMILITUDE (ver-ih-sih-MILL-ih-tood) *noun* — **having the appearance of truth**
Other forms: Verisimilar (*adj*); verisimilarly (*adv*)
Sentence: His story had the ring of *verisimilitude*, so we believed it.

VEX (VEKS) *verb* — **to cause mental torment; to trouble or distress**
Other forms: Vexation (*noun*); vexatious (*adj*); vexatiously (*adv*)
Sentence: I was so *vexed* by the error messages that I shut off the computer.

VICARIOUS (vy-KARE-ee-uss) *adj* — **acting as a substitute; in place of**
Other forms: Vicariously *(adv);* vicariousness (*noun*)
Sentence: Looking at their photos allowed us to enjoy a *vicarious* vacation.

VICISSITUDE (vih-SISS-ih-tood) *noun* — **fluctuation in luck or condition; obstacle**
Other form: Vicissitudinous (*adj*)
Sentence: They shared fifty years of both the joys and *vicissitudes* of marriage.

VIGILANT (VIJ-ih-lint) *adj* — **watchful; guarding**
Other forms: Vigil, vigilance (*nouns*); vigilantly (*adv*)
Sentence: It is difficult to be *vigilant* late at night, when the brain wants to sleep.

VINDICATE (VIN-dih-kayt) *verb* — **to free from guilt or blame; exculpate**
Other forms: Vindication (*noun*); vindicatory (*adj*)
Sentence: He had insisted he was innocent, and this new evidence *vindicated* him.

VINDICTIVE (vin-DIK-tiv) *adj* — **seeking revenge; vengeful; spiteful**
Other forms: Vindictively (*adv*); vindictiveness (*noun*)
Sentence: After the divorce, he remained angry and *vindictive* toward his ex-wife.

VIRTUOSO (ver-choo-OH-so) *noun* — **one who excels, especially in the arts; master**
Other forms: Virtuosity (*noun*); virtuoso (*adj*)
Sentence: Most of us were fairly competent with the violin, but he was a *virtuoso*.

VITIATE (VISH-ee-ayt) *verb* — **to spoil or corrupt; to injure; make incomplete**
Other forms: Vitiate (*adj*); vitiation (*noun*)
Sentence: Your dishonesty has *vitiated* the mutual trust we needed to work together.

VITRIOLIC (vich-ree-AHL-ik) *adj* — **harsh; biting; corrosive; caustic**
Other form: Vitriol (*noun*)
Sentence: My *vitriolic* outbursts got us all ejected from the courtroom.

VITUPERATE (vy-TOO-per-ayt) *verb* — **to scold strongly; berate**
Other forms: Vituperation (*noun*); vituperative (*adj*); vituperatively (*adv*)
Sentence: Teachers must correct and discipline students, but *vituperation* is unnecessary.

VIVACIOUS (vy-VAY-shuss) *adj* — **lively; spirited**
Other forms: Vivaciously (*adv*); vivaciousness, vivacity (*nouns*)
Sentence: How can such a *vivacious* woman be married to such a dull man?

VOCIFEROUS (vo-SIF-er-uss) *adj* — **prone to loud and forceful speech; boisterous**
    Other forms: Vociferously (*adv*); vociferousness (*noun*)
    Sentence: She was *vociferous* in her dissatisfaction with the job, complaining often.

VOLITION (vuh-LISH-un) *noun* — **an act of will; decisiveness**
    Other forms: Volitional (*adj*); volitionally (*adv*)
    Sentence: He was not kidnapped after all, but left by his own *volition*.

WARY (WARE-ee) *adj* — **cautious; prudent**
    Other forms: Warily (*adv*); wariness *(noun)*
    Sentence: We were *wary* of camping in the woods, but it's quite safe if you use your head.

WEAN (WEEN) *verb* — **to gradually deprive until a dependance is gone**
    Sentence: He knew he couldn't quit cold, so he *weaned* himself off the cigarettes.

WHET (WET) *verb* — **to arouse; stimulate**
    Sentence: The ad tries to *whet* your curiosity about the movie.

WHIMSICAL (WIM-zih-kul) *adj* — **unpredictable; fanciful; capricious**
    Other forms: Whim, whimsicality, whimsy (*nouns*); whimsically (*adv*)
    Sentence: You need to be a little more methodical, and a little less *whimsical*.

WINSOME (WIN-sum) *adj* — **pleasant; lighthearted; causing joy**
    Other forms: Winsomely (*adv*); winsomeness (*noun*)
    Sentence: The nurse had a *winsome* personality that always made her patients feel better.

WISTFUL (WIST-ful) *adj* — **tinged with sadness or yearning; melancholy**
    Other forms: Wistfully (*adv*); wistfulness (*noun*)
    Sentence: Her *wistful* smile betrayed some long-lost dream or disappointment.

ZEPHYR (ZEFF-er) *noun* — **a light, warm breeze**
    Sentence: A *zephyr* blew in from the west and it suddenly felt like spring.

Three more books by the same author:

14522233R10064

Made in the USA
Lexington, KY
03 April 2012